# NO BIGGER
## Than a Minute

# LOVE
## and HOPE
### Against All
### Odds

*A Memoir*

BY SHERI ROSE GENTRY

Gentry Wellness, LLC

No Bigger Than A Minute: Love and Hope Against All Odds
Pique Publishing, Inc.
San Diego, California U.S.A.

Library of Congress Control Number: 2022909428

GENTRY, SHERI, Author
NO BIGGER THAN A MINUTE: LOVE AND HOPE AGAINST ALL ODDS
SHERI GENTRY

Print ISBN: 978-0-578-33101-0
Digital ISBN: 978-0-578-33102-7

NONFICTION / Biography & Autobiography
NONFICTION / Body, Mind & Spirit

Editing and Book Design:
Nadia Geagea Pupa, Pique Publishing, Inc.

 Pique Publishing, Inc.

QUANTITY PURCHASES: Schools, companies, professional groups, clubs, and other organizations may qualify for special terms when ordering quantities of this title. For information, send a request via *gentrywellness@gmail.com*.

GentryWellness.com

To Georgette

# Foreword

L ife is made up of stories, and our stories matter. It is my deep desire that the story I share will ignite you to move forward in faith to impact humanity—even in the smallest way.

My story is my personal testimony: a witness to events and experiences that I cannot explain in the medical or even human realm. Sharing this story is a call on my life as an opportunity to create generational legacy.

As you read these words and envision the events in your mind's eye, it is my fervent desire that you recognize the higher power that is active in your life. This book is a tiny seed being planted in the fertile soil of hope. I hope it will propel you to step out of your comfort zone, walk in faith, and make a difference while on your earthly journey.

# Chapter One

t's the calm after the storm. The clinic is quiet and empty. Not so an hour ago. Waist-high tables with thin plastic pads were occupied by sick Haitian children and adults. The smell of sweaty bodies still lingers.

People travel miles to be seen by the missionary doctors and volunteers of the Hôpital Bon Samaritain in the valley village of Limbé, northern Haiti. For a moment, I sit on a dark green bench, normally tightly packed with ailing humanity. Although silent now, the cries, moans, and rapid-fire speech rings in my ears.

The room has five curtained cubicles, each large enough for one wooden exam table. The tile floor is scuffed from hundreds of weary feet in search of relief. A narrow hall at the end of the room leads to three similar rooms.

Sighing and wiping sweat off my neck, I decide to join the others for lunch—if anything is left. At the white porcelain sink, the cold water and handmade pink bar of soap strips the imperceptible filth from my hands and arms. I then walk a shadowed hall to my right leading to the green and white clinic door. A loud "click" and I know the dead bolt is secured.

*The staff endures a thankless job at this door during work hours. The pressure from so many wanting to get in while the staff resists their bribes and verbal abuse. . . .*

A girl moving toward me on the concrete walk interrupts my musings. She has a baby wrapped in soft cloth in her arms. Her steps hesitate and her eyes dart around the courtyard. There are four large trees that provide shade to the scattered cement benches that seat a few lingering visitors. The courtyard is flanked by the clinic in the front, the adult medical and maternity wards on the sides, and the round front of the pharmacy building at the far end. In the middle of the courtyard is a building large enough for two people. It is the *caisse*, the cashier's office, where patients pay for their visit to the clinic. At the far end of the maternity ward, across the walk from the pharmacy, is the ever-busy main mission office. A covered walk splits the courtyard and the adult medical ward. There are three dark dungeon-like rooms to the left of the walk and five larger rooms with four cots each to the right. The L-shaped pediatric wing is beyond the adult medical ward.

Approaching the girl with a baby, I ask, "Do you need something for the newborn? A vaccine?"

The girl is fourteen or fifteen years old, dressed in a pretty peach dress with flowers on it. She barely meets my gaze and gives a tiny nod.

*Lunch will wait. Who knows what they used to cut the umbilical cord?*

"Follow me. I will arrange for the shot," I reply.

*I never want to experience another baby die a painful death from tetanus. It is so unnecessary.*

I unlock the dead bolt. Her shuffling shoes scrape on the cement hall floor as she follows.

A worn journal for documenting birth information is on the corner of the small wooden consultation table. "I have some questions and then will give you a ticket for the shot. The nurse in maternity will give the vaccine to the baby."

No response. Not even a nod.

"Male or female?"

"Female." Just above a whisper.

"Time of birth?"

"Early this morning, before sunrise."

"Parents' names?"

"Assondier Rémy. Elirose Menard Rémy."

"Where do they live? What village?"

"Camp Coq, 4th district."

*Hmmm. That's a distance to travel. No wonder she missed the clinic hours.*

The girl fidgets from one foot to the other. Fear is in her eyes as I reach toward the bundle in her arms.

"I'm going to check the baby and weigh her for the record book. I'm almost done."

One layer of soft cloth. Then another, and another. Finally, I see her.

"Oh my." My head snaps up to look at the girl. "She's tiny!"

The girl quickly looks away and nervously bounces the baby in her arms. It is immediately obvious: this is a premature baby. Black, silky hair covers the sleeping baby's head. Fine, downy hair extends onto her face. Her head is only the size of a small orange.

Ever so gently, I remove the baby from the blankets. Her body fits in one hand. Carefully, I place her on the infant scale and wait for the needle to adjust. "Three pounds, one ounce." Swiftly, I scoop up this miniature bit of humanity. As I rewrap her, my heart is pounding in my ears. *God, what am I to do now?*

"There is more to this story. I need to know the rest of the story."

In a jumble of Creole words that I can barely follow, the girl begins to cry. "My sister, the mother of this baby, is dying. She is dying on the mountain." A pitiful moaning cry emerges from the cloth bundle. "Please, you must take the baby."

Lunch is long forgotten as I try to get more information. A torrent of hysterical exclamations pours out. I can only snatch a few words. "Fever . . . baby born early . . . seven months . . . can't breathe . . . dying." Suddenly, she thrusts the bundle toward me. "Please, you are her only chance."

Logic and emotion collide within me.

"This is a hospital. Bring the mother here. This baby needs her mother. She needs mother's milk. Otherwise, her chance to live is small."

She closes her eyes for a long moment and sucks in a deep breath. When she opens her sad eyes and looks directly into mine, I realize she thinks I don't understand a word she said. Slowly, she repeats, "The mother's on the mountain. She's dying. There's no way to bring her. It'll cost too much. She's dying, do you understand? She may already be gone."

Reluctantly, I accept the bundle and cradle the wisp of life in my arm. In that microsecond, although I am not consciously aware, life shifts for me. My desire to fix all things before me and the where-there's-a-will-there's-a-way attitude takes over me. I reach into my smock pocket and pull out a couple Haitian gourds, the common paper money.

*I didn't know why I put those in there this morning. Now, I do.* I press the money into the distraught girl's hands.

"Find a way to get her here. We'll do all we can for her."

She brushes at her tear-streaked face. Then, she tenderly touches the bundle. She turns and is gone in a flash.

*That may be the last time I see her or the money.*

I peek at the tiny, little face looking up at me from the cloths. Her eyes are open. They seem to be the biggest part of her. She has round little cheeks and pink cherub-like lips. Instinctively, I begin to gently rock her in my arms.

"What are we going to do now, little one?" I take a deep breath. My options are limited. As I gaze at her magnetic eyes, I leave the clinic. Securing the lock, my mind reels.

*I wonder if the girl intended to abandon the baby at the clinic door as others have done. Maybe she meant to arrive late.*

It is a dozen steps to the door of the maternity ward. As I enter from the bright tropical sunlight, one Haitian nurse and two aides turn to look at me with surprise.

"What do you have there, Madame Rich?"

I'm aware of the sweat running down my temple and know it has more to do with the situation than the temperature.

"I'm admitting this baby to the hospital."

The nurse chuckles. "Madame Rich, have you been gone too long from us? You need to admit the baby to the pediatric ward."

I step closer and reveal the baby's tiny face. Three sets of eyes peer in and, collectively, they look at me with shock.

"It's too small."

"Born too early."

"Oh, good God, no hope."

"I'm going to put her in the incubator," I say with determination.

Once again, the nurse shakes her head and makes a "tsk" clicking sound with her tongue. "Madame Rich, the incubator is broken. It's been weeks since we put a baby in there."

Wooden, floor-to-ceiling file drawers separate the delivery area from the nurses' desk. Rounding the corner, I see the familiar delivery beds with metal-leg supports. The two delivery beds are a mere two feet apart. The incubator is against the far wall, a few feet from the end of the beds. A flat table with a thin, lime-green, plastic-covered pad is parallel to the delivery beds, to clean and dress newborns.

I recall the first time I took responsibility for overseeing the maternity ward when I was here between 1984 and 1986.

*   *   *   *

The missionary nurse left that morning for a year-long furlough. Leading up to her departure, I had shadowed her and delivered a couple of babies under her watchful eye.

On that same morning after she left, I was greeted with anxious Haitian nurses and a cacophony of five moaning and yelling women in labor. One woman showed a baby's head crowning. I hurriedly put on a pair of gloves and guided the newborn into the world. The cord was cut and tied, and I barely handed the newborn to the aide when the next mother let out a scream.

Another head appeared. There was barely enough time to change gloves from the first patient. I struggled but successfully got the first pair of gloves off while the nurse got in the woman's face.

"Breathe. Don't push."

The woman ignored the instructions, propelling the shoulders through the birth canal. Barehanded, I caught the baby not a moment too soon.

*That was close.* I wiped bloody, sticky hands on my smock.

Noticing a large amount of blood coming from the first woman, I put on the first pair of gloves. *Waste not, want not.*

I delivered the afterbirth and deeply massaged her floppy uterus to control the hemorrhage. As I stitched a laceration, the nurse delivered the second patient's afterbirth.

It was total chaos.

The aides had no place to clean and dress the newborns. A third mother was on the flat table, rolling from side to side. On the other side of the aisle, a shorter table—normally used for supplies and a baby scale—was also occupied with a moaning and laboring woman. I had to step carefully over the fifth woman who was on a mat on the floor.

*What have I agreed to do here?*

There was little time to consider or fret as the onslaught continued. I later laughed about my initiation rites to the maternity ward. That turned out to be an unusual day. There would be many more opportunities for new life and chaos in this small part of the room, but never five in active labor simultaneously.

*    *    *    *

I carefully lay the premature newborn on the table so I can examine her more closely. I warm the head of my stethoscope in my hands. It's obviously too large for her chest. Her belly pumps up and down to help her rib-showing lungs to breathe. Everything seems to be intact, only miniature with signs of being two months premature. I wrap her again in the cloths and walk over to the ancient, leaded-glass, steel-cased incubator.

Another memory flashes to the surface as I recall a set of triplets. The first baby was born in the dirt on the way to the hospital and arrived with the umbilical cord still attached and hanging from the mother, who walked the remainder of the way. All three babies stayed in this one incubator. None of them lived.

Frustrated, yet again, at the lack of even the most basic equipment, I am determined to *de-gagé*—make do with what I have. I fiddle with the machine. No luck. *It's probably electrical.*

"What's Doc think about this?" a nurse asks from behind me, referring to Dr. Hodges.

"I haven't told him yet. This happened after everyone went for lunch. Besides, isn't Dr. Steve on-call for emergencies this afternoon? Will you send someone for him, please?"

"Yes, Madame Rich."

"What will Miss Cheryl say?" asks the aide, curiously watching me examine the baby.

Cheryl is a volunteer nurse in her twenties from the States. She has been here for six months and now oversees the maternity ward. My responsibility this term is to get the new surgical ward functional. I also help in the outpatient clinic as much as possible. I have only been back for a few weeks, and I do not know everyone well.

"I can tell you, she won't be happy."

"What choice do I have?"

I turn and look at the nurse whose eyes speak the words her mouth does not—*it's hopeless anyway.*

I place the baby in the incubator.

*Maybe simply being in the confined space will help maintain her precious body temperature.*

I ask the nurse to label her inpatient chart as "Bebé Rémy." A newborn with no name.

Dr. Steve arrives and I explain the situation to him. He examines her.

"She's certainly a small one. I am not sure we've had success with any her size. She is at risk for hypothermia."

"The nurses just told me the incubator is broken. I can't get it to work."

"Monitoring her temperature is very important. We have to see who can fix the incubator. She's also at risk for dehydration and sepsis." Sepsis is a widespread infection.

He writes orders for the vaccine and antibiotic drops. He orders a feeding schedule every three hours using the formula from a Japanese company, Morinaga.

*An unusual set of circumstances has come together at this time to provide life to a most unlikely soul.*

Dr. Steve and I leave the ward and walk together to Dr. Hodges' house in the middle of the mission compound. All the volunteers have eaten and gone. I hesitantly explain the admission of the premature baby to the maternity ward and ask if anything can be done about the incubator problem.

Dr. Hodges is sixty-four years old and has been working at Hôpital Bon Samaritain since it was only a small outpatient clinic in 1953. With silver-gray hair on his balding head, he is a man of great compassion. He understands this culture and the people well.

"She will not survive. They never do; not at that size. We don't have all the capabilities you enjoy in the States to support such an undertaking."

Even so, he calls out the screened window to Jacques, a wiry Haitian yard worker.

"Go over to the shop and see if there's someone who can fix the incubator in maternity." Looking at me with a half chuckle, he says, "You see why I call you Alice, as in Alice in Wonderland? You are always such an idealist."

*And what is wrong with that?* I become engrossed with my dusty tennis shoes.

"You'll want to find Cheryl and tell her the new responsibility you've arranged for her."

# Chapter Two

Gray cinder block walls and poured cement pillars are getting a coat of paint. These empty rooms of the new surgical ward will soon house many recovering patients. We expect several short-term surgical mission teams. At this moment, the surgical ward is a virtually blank slate of possibility. I divide my time between tasks for readying the ward and support staff and providing consultations in the outpatient clinic.

As I rummage through a storage room with hand-built wooden shelves, I discover several prize instruments—cast-offs from an unknown surgery unit. I hurry to my dear friend, Madame Abner, who I find in the new sterilization room. She's carefully wiping the recently installed donated unit. It's much larger than the autoclaves we have for the main hospital.

"Madame Abner, look what I found. These are instruments we can put into a pack for an emergency exploratory surgery."

She flashes a big grin and her eyes twinkle. She tilts her head slightly to the right to see me clearly. Since birth, her right eye does not line up evenly with her left, though I don't even notice this particular trait anymore. I adore her happy spirit and am grateful for our long talks. She's always been patient with my attempts to speak Creole, often teaching me a better phrase.

"Madame Rich, you remember the language well, even though you have been gone from us. You must visit my house soon and see Adlin. He's talking a lot these days, too."

Adlin is near and dear to my heart. He was an orphan in the hospital nursery during my previous volunteer term. I'd play with him on my free afternoons. At that time, he was known as "Ti Jacques." He had big round cheeks, a melt-your-heart smile, and curly black hair. He was a happy baby and in good health. When he was about a year old, he was chosen to move to the larger orphanage in the capital city, Port-au-Prince. From there, the hope for adoption by a foreign family was greater.

"It'll be so difficult when they take Ti Jacques to Port. I won't know what becomes of him," I remember telling Madame Abner.

"I know. He's special."

During one of our talks, Madame Abner shared her longing to have a family. Unfortunately, she had undergone an emergency hysterectomy a few years earlier. Her husband, Abner, a deacon in the Limbé Baptist Church, also desperately wanted children. He knew they would never have their own.

One day, an epiphany struck me. Ti Jacques needed a family; Madame Abner and her husband wanted children. A natural connection was evident when I brought him to visit her in the hospital sterilization room above the pharmacy.

"Madame Abner, you and your husband should adopt Ti Jacques. He loves you. And it's clear you adore him."

She abruptly stopped playing with him and handed him back to me. "No. We cannot adopt a child."

Confused by the flash of pain and longing in her eyes, I asked, "Why not? He's healthy."

She looked at me to decide if I would understand what she was about to say. "In our culture, it's not good to adopt someone's child. You don't know what problems it has."

"You mean like illness or birth defects?"

She hesitated. "No, I mean evil. Or curses placed on the child."

I was astounded. The pervasive spiritual significance impacted everyone.

Time grew closer to his departure. Madame Abner was more attached than ever to Ti Jacques. I continued to encourage adoption. We talked and prayed about it.

One day, as I was walking to the hospital, Madame Abner called to me from the top of the stairs by the main hospital sterilization room. Her energy was pure excitement. "Madame Rich, I have news for you!"

She hurried down the steps and threw her arms around me. When she let go, she danced in front of me. "Abner and I talked about Ti Jacques. We are looking for God's answer."

"And did you get an answer? You're very happy today."

"Yes. We're Christian believers. God is stronger than any evil forces. We're taking Ti Jacques as our own!"

Another hug. My excitement in that moment matched hers.

"Abner spoke with Miss Barbara already this morning. She'll help with the papers. Ti Jacques is not going to Port."

Barbara is one of the Hodges' grown children. She'd been through the adoption process several times. The doctor and his wife, Joanna, had taken children with special needs to bring up as their own.

"I'm so happy for you. I'm happy for Ti Jacques. He was meant to be yours."

Weeks later, I walked with Madame Abner through the streets of Limbé. Although the adoption was not complete, they were permitted to take Ti Jacques home. I carried a bag of donated clothes and toys. Every few feet, she stopped to show off her new son to everyone who had the slightest interest. She beamed. They gave him a new name, Adlin. He was excited, too. The new parents decided they would not tell him he was adopted. Instead, they would rear him as if he was their biological child.

Now, I consider what a blessing it is to have this dear friend. It doesn't seem like two years have passed with me in the States. Our friendship resumes from where it was.

"I will most certainly come and visit you, Abner, and Adlin."

"You'll be surprised. You won't have as long a walk. We moved to a house within the village."

"I can hardly wait to see—"

*CRASH!*

We hear several excited men's voices. We rush through the main surgical doors and to the room on the right to see what happened. A wooden ladder is on its side next to the domed fixture of our only surgical light.

"What happened? Is everyone all right?" I ask.

"Yes, Madame Rich. I told him it was too heavy to carry up the ladder."

Looking at TiRo, a lanky young man whose pride seems most bruised, I ask, "Are you hurt?"

"No, I'm good. We'll have to put the parts back together."

"Let's find a safer way to install that light, or you may be our first surgical patient when you break something." Everyone laughs and the tension is broken.

There's much to do for this facility to be functional. The need is huge. Currently, if a woman needs an emergency C-section, a driver transports her in one of the mission vehicles. The government hospital in Cap-Haïtien is the destination. Oftentimes, the hour-long trip doesn't have a good outcome.

Other surgical emergencies also present themselves. I remember my first week ever at the hospital. I was making rounds with Dr. Hodges. A young man was in the adult medical ward with IV fluid running. He had a ruptured appendix that formed a pus-filled abscess in his abdomen. I was shocked.

"Shouldn't he have surgery?"

"Surgery isn't an option here. Either he'll get better slowly with the antibiotics or he'll die."

To my utter amazement, he lived. Weeks after being admitted, he walked out of the hospital. The practice of medicine here is a creative art.

I leave the surgical ward and detour to maternity on my way to the clinic. I take a shortcut through the orphan room. This is where I first met Adlin. The babies and toddlers arrive here through many different circumstances. Several have developmental or physical handicaps. Others were left abandoned for unknown reasons.

An aide wearing a green apron feeds a baby. I smile at her. "I'll visit and play with the babies on my afternoon off."

"Yes, Ma Rich."

I step into maternity and find Cheryl at the nurses' desk. As predicted, she wasn't pleased with the "hopeless" baby in the now-functioning incubator.

"It's so frustrating to find a way to feed her. And it takes so much time. One of the aides has to spend an hour or two with a dropper or spoon. The bottle nipples are too big for her mouth."

I move to the incubator to see Bebé Rémy through the glass top. Her little arms are waving about as she looks up with wide open eyes. Such hopeful eyes.

"For being so little, you sure are vigorous." I marvel that she's even still alive.

"Dr. Steve stopped in. He is worried about her hydration and a low-grade fever."

A noisy throng of people wait outside the clinic door. They are the "lucky" ones with a ticket to be seen and have already accomplished several steps. A clinic visit begins in a large pavilion outside the hospital entrance. Every morning, a lay pastor leads a short devotional. One of the doctors then triages the hundreds of waiting people. Although a few hundred will be seen today, many still are turned away. It's a stressful start. *I'm glad I never have to do triage. How to choose?*

A large waiting room filled with worn wooden benches is a temporary holding place. Patients who have a rendezvous ticket for a follow-up from a previous visit approach one of two small windows. Those with a new triage ticket approach another. The din is nearly deafening. Staff in the chart rooms locate or make new outpatient charts. These are sheets of half-yellow card stock with a record for payments on the front. When the charts are ready, the patients line up at the clinic door to await controlled admittance.

As I wade through packed bodies, my nose is assaulted by rank odors of dirty clothes, flesh, and sour vomit. *The Haitians have a much smaller personal space than I prefer. Mouth breathe.*

Finally getting to the door, I am greeted by Aduthene with a huge smile. His closely shaved head is six inches over most of the people waiting.

He yells, "Step back from the door." He manhandles the door against un-moving bodies so I can squeeze through.

*Getting through the door is like a baby getting through a birth canal.*

I walk through the front consultation area and arrive at the alcove where I see patients. It has two six-foot tables, each with half-inch foam pads covered with colorful plastic. There is a wooden step to make it easier for patients to get on the tables. Cloth curtains hang from suspended rods and separate the exam areas from each other and the room. A two-by-three-foot wooden table is my desk for writing. There is a sink and two woven chairs. The first of the fifty or more patients I will evaluate are lined shoulder to shoulder on a bench against the wall. The entire space is about eight-by-eight feet and has open louvered glass windows on two sides. My nurse for the day barks at the first two patients, "You. Get on the table."

I work through the morning asking questions and examining patients to determine their ailments. Over my lightweight cotton floral dress, I wear a standard pale-blue, waist-length smock. It ties in the back and has three large pockets across the front. I keep two pens and a roll of medical tape in one pocket. Tucked in the middle pocket, though I rarely need to use it now, is a list of common Creole terms appropriate for the clinic setting. In the left pocket is a roll of "bandage"—the four-inch strips of old sheets that have been lovingly rolled by volunteer groups in the States. It has a variety of uses and I cannot imagine working without it. By midmorning, a V-shaped sweat mark is noticeable at my chest.

I decide appropriate treatments. I order tests to be done in our little laboratory or X-ray department. Malaria, typhoid, parasites, headaches, tuberculosis, diabetes, and a host of other disorders are routine for the day.

It's nearly 11:00 a.m. when I hear Dr. Hodges speaking with the nurse outside the curtained cubicle. Peeking inside, he clears his throat and says, "If you have a moment, I think you should come with me."

I quickly finish with the patient on the table and follow. He slides a curtain aside and I see an ill-appearing woman lying on the exam table. Every breath is a struggle. A stoic, sweating man observes anxiously from the corner.

"I can't believe it. This is the mother of that premature baby you admitted on Saturday." Tipping his head toward the man. "This is her husband. He carried her down the mountain on his back."

I meet the man's watchful gaze and turn my attention to the woman. It is obvious she's critically ill.

"She has a fever of 103°F. She's in congestive heart failure. I'm admitting her to the maternity ward immediately. On the way, she will need a chest X-ray and blood work." Looking at me, he finishes, "I thought you would want to know."

"May I quickly examine her also?"

"Help yourself. You'll find a heart murmur like you've never heard before."

He's right. I almost do not need a stethoscope to hear the loud rushing sound coming from her enlarged heart. Poor air movement in her lungs indicates they are filled with fluid. Her tight and protuberant belly is also fluid filled. Her liver is massive and firm. She exhibits significant swelling in her legs, with ankles larger than my thighs. Her breathing is rapid and shallow, and while she's not comatose, she's working too hard for every breath to be able to speak. Her half-opened eyes are glassy.

With a heavy heart, I return to my consultation area.

*She's really sick. I wonder what we'll be able to do for her.*

My next patient is sitting on the table with her legs extended. She appears to be about fifty years old. Her matted hair is wild on her head, and she stares straight ahead.

"What problem do you have?"

No response. Unblinking stare.

"Madame, can you hear me?"

Still no response.

I turn to the family member who is with her. "Can you tell me why she's here?"

"She has a zombie."

"A zombie? What do you mean?" I feel her skin and it is warm. Pinching her arm does not elicit a flinch.

"There was white powder across the door, and she stepped in it. She has a zombie."

Further questions do not get me any closer to a diagnosis. I ask the nurse to get one of the doctors. A few minutes later, Dr. Hodges appears.

"What's the problem?"

"The only thing the family will say is she has a 'zombie.' She sits and stares and I can't get any response."

He turns to the family member. "What's the story?"

A second family member enters the cubicle, and both begin rapidly explaining to Dr. Hodges about a curse and the powder.

Placing his stethoscope on her chest, he looks at me and says, "Order a Widal for typhoid."

*How did he determine that?*

I finish seeing my morning patients, but the baby's sick mother is never far from my thoughts.

Rich, my husband, joins me at home for lunch. The house we now occupy belongs to a family who are on furlough for most of the year. Rich and I met on this mission compound in 1984. We were volunteers supported by different Ohio churches. Much of our friendship blossomed during the midweek bible studies and Friday game nights held in this very home. Although Rich returned to the States at the completion of his one-year commitment, I stayed for a second year.

Rich's responsibility, then and now, is overseeing the pharmacy. He is not medically trained but does an excellent job of keeping records. He monitors all supplies for the hospital. He also tabulates the charts at the end of each clinic day. Four or five Haitians work at windows at the round front of the building. They fill prescriptions written by the providers in the clinic.

"The mother of the premature baby was brought in today. She's very ill," I tell him.

"Is the baby still alive?"

"Amazingly."

An added bonus with this house is Madame Edmond. She is the house-keeper for the family and agreed to work for us. She is soft-spoken and smiles a lot. Her eyes twinkle behind large eyeglasses. "I made sandwiches from eggs and the can of tuna. I also bought you three ripe mangoes and sliced one for your lunch."

Rejuvenated by a meal and rest period, I return to the clinic. The standard operating function of the clinic is a controlled chaos to the uninitiated. People of all ages appear. I see effects of delayed treatment. Often, people have used their resources at the witch doctor before finally coming to the hospital. Although I do not know the significance, many little children have a chicken beak or dog tooth charm on a thin string around their neck. I've learned that a tight cloth tied around a head with leaves means the person has a headache. A tight-knotted band around the abdomen means the person almost always has parasites. These are things I could never learn from a textbook.

The consultations continue throughout the afternoon. The morning patients return with lab results. The person whose family could only tell me she "had a zombie" has a positive test for typhoid fever. I admit her to the adult medical ward so she can receive antibiotic injections.

Slowly, we clear the patients from the clinic. A few of the Haitian staff are gathered and laughing together. It is good to see them enjoying themselves after the tension of the day.

Leaving through the now-vacant clinic door, I note the line is still twelve deep at the two windows of the caisse. After paying a small amount for their visit and medications, those patients still need to go to the pharmacy. It looks like Rich will be awhile before he is done.

"Sheri."

I stop. The Haitians refer to me as Madame Rich, which is appropriate for a married woman. I was "Miss Sheri" as a single woman my first trip. I glance around to see who called me. Dr. Hodges is walking toward me from the pediatric ward area. I wait for him.

"I had to perform a thoracentesis on the premature baby's mother." It's a procedure to drain fluid out of her chest cavity. "I expect she'll need more procedures like that if she lives."

"What do you think caused her to be so sick?"

"I suspect rheumatic fever. Maybe also TB. She needs open-heart surgery for the heart valve and we both know she'll not get that."

Since Rich is delayed, I decide to return to the maternity ward. In the delivery area, a woman is in labor. An aide spoons formula to Bebé Remy. Both are wearing more than what gets in her mouth.

My tired feet turn to the large ward room. There are eight beds side by side on the two long walls. Passing through the center aisle, I come to the second, smaller room which only has four beds. Here, I find the baby's mother. Her family is gathered. Two of the women are engaged in animated conversation. One is her mother, the other her mother-in-law. They stop talking and watch as I check her pulse. They do not ask me about the mother or the baby's condition.

"What's that in her arm?"

"That's serum. We are giving her medicine in this so it can work quickly."

They seem wary. In hushed tones, they discuss her condition as "grave," as expected. I note that the patient is less labored in her breathing. Her eyes are open and clearer.

"Is it easier for you to breathe after the doctor removed the fluid?"

Resigned eyes momentarily connect with mine. "Yes."

# Chapter Three

"I can't get that little baby off my mind," I tell Rich as we finish breakfast and have prayer time. "No one can believe she's still alive."

"She's sure a tiny little thing," he agrees. "How's Cheryl handling the extra responsibility?"

"I think she's stressed. There's more going on for her than work." I clear the breakfast dishes. "I'm going to the hospital a little early so I can see how everyone did through the night."

Madame Edmond enters the house as I am leaving. "I'm doing laundry today. Do you have the basket ready for me?"

"Yes. It's already on the side porch by the washer."

We take simple chores like laundry for granted in the States. We're thrilled this house has a washing machine. Previously, our laundry was done with the other volunteers and missionaries. The hospital employs "wash ladies" who carry large woven baskets on their heads to the Limbé River. The clothes are washed by hand in the river and laid to dry in the sun on the shoreline.

Madame Edmond will hang our clothes to dry on the lines near the house. Electricity can be intermittent, so I hope she'll able to finish a load. The hospital has a large backup generator in the event of an electrical outage, but it only powers the critical needs of the hospital.

I hurry along the cement walk. *I sure am glad for these sidewalks in the rainy season.*

With this being early September, we can expect tropical storms and hurricanes at any time. I take three steps up to the elevated walk that connects the buildings of the hospital.

Suddenly, Joanna Hodges bursts out of the main office door nearly running into me. "Oh, there you are. I think we have a problem in the maternity ward."

Immediately, I'm on high alert as she falls in step beside me. Concern for the premature baby or her mother is foremost in my mind.

"Actually, we learned that Cheryl left last night."

"What? Where'd she go?"

"No one seems to know. Her cottage roommate said she was gone when she woke up. This isn't the best time to be going off on one's own, so I hope she's safe." Joanna begins a lively conversation with the Haitians on duty.

"She told us she needed time away—a vacation."

"Did she say where she was going? When she'll be back?"

"No, Madame Doctor."

The screen door squeaks. Dr. Hodges steps up into the nurses' station. He clears his throat in his characteristic way. "So, what's happening here?"

Joanna quickly recounts what she knows. One arm is across his chest and the other hand slowly stroking his chin. "Hmm. When do we expect more volunteers?"

"There are four coming for the Christmas holidays. Cheryl was expecting to take a break then. So are Rich and Sheri."

Slowly, he casts his pale-blue eyes toward me. "I know you have much work in surgery and the clinic. You do have experience with overseeing this ward. Would you help here until we know if Cheryl's returning or if another volunteer's coming?"

Eagerly, I smile and nod affirmative. "I'd be happy to. Although, I may not have as much time to help in the clinic." A rush surges through me. The opportunity to again participate in the miracle of new life fills me with awe and angst simultaneously.

Together, Dr. Hodges and I review the inpatient charts of the women in the ward. Meanwhile, Joanna gets called away to solve a problem with rations for pediatrics. We visit each patient and adjust orders. We plan to discharge two new mothers. Arriving at the bed of Madame Assondier, Dr. Hodges bends over to examine her. She has less swelling than previously. Her breathing is rapid and shallow.

"She needs more fluid drained from her lungs today. And possibly her abdomen. Do you want to perform those procedures here or in the clinic?"

"It'll be easier for her if I do the thoracentesis and paracentesis right here."

I make a mental note of the equipment I need to gather.

"It's good you'll be working here. Cheryl isn't comfortable doing procedures like those. You have the experience."

After informing the nurse of the orders and patients we want released, I go to the incubator. The tiny baby is shivering. *She's cold. What's wrong with this machine?*

I open the top and lift the crying baby out of her glass cocoon. The heat knob is turned down. She is also wet. The ever-versatile "bandage" are her diapers. Since the sheet material isn't absorbent, she needs changing often. The newborn size T-shirt is like an oversized overcoat on the fragile frame of this little one; it's wet too.

Dr. Hodges shakes his head. "She won't survive." His stark statement is spoken with assurance of years of experience in this land of loss. I do not agree, but have too much respect for Dr. Hodges to debate him. I ask the aide to find another small shirt while I check her condition. Big, brown, hopeful eyes look up at me.

"I guess you and I will be seeing more of each other."

# Chapter Four

The gravity of the new responsibility begins to settle on me. After the morning rounds through the maternity ward, I stop to check on Bebé Rémy. I turn to the nurse.

"How's the baby with breastfeeding?"

She shakes her head sadly. "The mother's too sick and the baby's too small to take anything."

I check the incubator and find that the heat knob has been turned down again. "Who keeps turning down the heat?" *I'm going to set this and put tape over it so no one can change it.*

I remove the little elastic cap from the baby's head and carefully stroke her fontanel—the soft spot on the top of her head. It is slightly depressed, indicating her hydration status is less than ideal. Looking through her chart, I notice incomplete record keeping.

"Madame Tony, please make sure the temperature's recorded in the chart every six hours as the order's written. It's important. The record shows it being done once a day or less."

"Yes, Madame Rich. We get busy here with all the pregnant ladies and the ones who have delivered. Sometimes, we don't have enough people to do everything for that baby."

I am concerned. Bebé Rémy's need for hydration is greater than the difficulty of feeding her. Everyone's too busy. I pick her up and sit in the rocking chair in the corner of the room. Again, her big, dark eyes cause my heart to skip a beat. *If I could read what those eyes are saying, it'd be, "Please help me."*

The aide hands me her bottle. "Madame Rich, you see, the bottle nipple is so big for her." Indeed, the nipple is twice the size it should be for her tiny mouth.

"Have you checked with the Miss La Foi in pediatrics to see if they have a smaller one?"

"I'll go see, Madame Rich."

Tiny dry lips open to accept the dropper offered. She makes a half-hearted attempt to suck at it. Her skin is more wrinkled. Skin turgor is an important indication of her hydration, and it is poor. A few drops at a time.

The aide returns empty handed. "They don't have smaller nipples either. I also checked with Madame Doctor to see if she knew where we can get smaller ones. She said she'd try."

I stand and take Bebé Rémy to the scale. Madame Tony is a tall and broad-shouldered woman. She joins me.

"Two pounds, twelve ounces."

Madame Tony records the weight in the chart. "That's her lowest weight yet."

*Oh, Lord.* My thoughts are racing. *This trend cannot continue.* My conversation with God begins silently in my head and my heart.

*Why is this happening, Lord? What am I supposed to do?*

No booming voices. Heaven is silent. I remember another desperate time I pleaded with God for answers.

The country was Mexico. It was a required academic term abroad. I was a physician assistant student on an internship in a small dispensary. Mexico was not my first choice of locations and I felt inadequate to communicate in a foreign language. I was dreadfully ill and was convinced I'd die there. On my bed late one night, with a fever of 105°F, I had a conversation with God. It was more like a one-sided argument.

*Why is this happening? Why did you bring me to this place? To die? I miss my family and friends. Will I ever see them again?* I ranted until exhaustion overtook me. Then, I recalled a discussion with a friend about prayer.

"You need to listen when you pray. It's a conversation between two people."

I waited. No booming voices from heaven. *What would God say if I was to hear His response?* In the stillness of my heart, I heard the answer to my questions: *I don't do anything without a reason. Look for the reason I have you there.*

The next day, my roommate discovered that antibiotics were available without a prescription. In a few days, I was strong enough to return to the dispensary. We gave vaccinations and changed wound dressings. One particularly poor and toothless beggar woman touched my heart. She insisted I take her gift of a precious coin in gratitude for my care. That's when I realized I had talents to serve the less fortunate of the world. She represented the reason I was in Mexico.

From that moment on, I looked for a way to serve in a third-world country as a physician assistant. Specifically, I searched for a paid position in a Spanish-speaking country. I wrote to fifty-four different organizations seeking an opportunity. A prayer request shared at my home church, Painesville First Baptist Church in Ohio, asked for additional medical providers; it had me thinking God has a sense of humor. He gave me the opportunity to work in Haiti on a silver platter. It was a volunteer position and the language, a dialect of French.

I am absolutely certain of His calling. Looking down at this tiny baby, I pray God will guide my care for her. I hope He will reveal the reason she is even still alive.

Suddenly, there is a tremendous commotion at the door. I quickly place the baby in the incubator. Several men carry in a pregnant woman. She appears nearly unconscious. I notice she's bleeding profusely and suspect she's in shock.

"Put her on this delivery table. You," I say, pointing to the aide, "Go get a doctor from the clinic right now. Madame Tony, get a delivery kit and gloves for me and the doctor."

I shout to another hospital worker, who comes to see what the excitement is all about, "Go to the pharmacy and get a serum and tubing. Tell Rich it's an emergency."

"Shhhhh!" I strain to hear fetal heart tones with the old-fashioned fetoscope. We do not have a Doppler—an electronic device used to detect heart tones. We also do not have an ultrasound. These are basic equipment in the States, but not here. The woman moans and crescendos to a scream as a contraction grips her midsection. I can't hear any heart tones. Waving my free hand again for quiet, I adjust the location and listen. Another hospital worker arrives and moves people out of the area.

Madame Tony gathers the items requested and she manages to get a blood pressure cuff on a flailing arm.

"There is too much blood. She is hemorrhaging. Where is the doctor?"

At that moment, I hear the door slam. Dr. Steve makes his way through the noisy crowd gathered by the nurses' desk. Behind him is the aide with the intravenous fluid, tubing, and needle to place it. Dr. Steve stops and faces the crowd. He gestures for silence.

"Who's with this woman?"

People speak all at once. A thin man steps forward, leaning on an older woman.

"She's my madame. This is her mother."

"Tell me what happened."

"She had a lot of blood and became indisposed."

"When?"

"Earlier this morning. We got a tap-tap right away." A tap-tap is a common form of mass transit in Haiti. It is usually a small, brightly painted truck with seats in the bed, with more people packed in it than there are available seats.

While Dr. Steve tries to get more information from the family, I continue to search for heart tones. Her vital signs support my diagnosis of shock. He joins me and I quickly give him my findings.

Quietly, I tell him, "I am afraid the baby is gone. I can't hear heart tones."

He quickly dons gloves and moves to the end of the table.

"It'll be difficult, but you must get an IV placed."

With the rubber tourniquet on her arm, I feel for a vein. With a soothing calm voice, I tell her, "We're helping you. I have to poke your arm to give you medicine. *Kem-be fem*. Hold strong."

Under his breath, Dr. Steve says, "The placenta detached either partially or completely. I'm sure the baby's dead. We must get her delivered or we'll lose her, too. There's not enough time to transport her to Cap-Haïtien."

Her veins are nearly non-existent with all the blood she lost. *Lord, help me get this*. I insert the needle in her arm. Amazingly, I get it on the first attempt. Madame Tony hands me tape to secure it as another wave of pain shudders through the woman.

Dr. Steve instructs the aide, "Go get Dr. Hodges from the clinic and use the back door. Hurry." To another, he instructs, "Get someone from the lab here to get her blood count and blood type, stat. Take members of her family to see if they have a matching blood type."

I update Dr. Steve with her vital signs every couple of minutes. I note that her abdomen is hard like a rock and that she drifts in and out of consciousness.

Dr. Hodges makes his way through the crowd and tells them they must wait outside. Dr. Steve quickly and calmly explains the situation to him.

Dr. Hodges checks the woman himself. "I agree. You don't have the luxury of time on your side to take her to the government hospital. Your only option is to deliver. You'll need the forceps."

"The head is not in a low enough position to do forceps safely." Dr. Steve's forehead is creased with worry and he's sweating. "I considered that already."

"It's your only option, all things considered. Can you handle this? I have a woman in the clinic that was hit by a *camion*. She's got a compound leg fracture."

"Sure. I'll let you know how this goes."

The next ten minutes are a blur. Dr. Steve applies the forceps and pulls. Readjust. Pull. Madame Tony and I hold her in position and instruct her to push. Her efforts are weak.

Finally, a blue and floppy baby boy is extracted. Dr. Steve cuts and clamps the cord. He takes him to the table and checks for breathing. None. He calls for an Ambu bag, meant for an adult, and instructs the aide how to operate it.

"Can you get the epinephrine from the emergency kit?" he asks Madame Tony.

Dr. Steve feels for a heartbeat. None. With his two fingers he starts chest compressions. As soon as Madame Tony has it ready, the epinephrine is injected into the heart. No response. The baby is gone.

While Dr. Steve works on the baby, I take care of the woman. The placenta was delivered with the baby, confirming the suspicion of placental abruption. For the forceps, Dr. Steve had to make a large episiotomy. I repair it.

The dead newborn is wrapped by the aide.

Dr. Steve asks the family back into the nurses' station. "We did everything possible. The baby boy probably died before you arrived at the hospital." Looking at the woman's husband, "Your madame lost a lot of blood. She is alive and very weak. Is someone giving blood for her?"

"Yes. Her brother is in the laboratory."

"The undertaker will take the body and bury it before the end of the day," Madame Tony explains.

He nods but seems emotionally disconnected. The aide gets a box from Rich so the body can be placed in it. Only the woman's mother requests to see the baby.

I take her to the table where the baby is wrapped.

"Oh Lord, oh Lord," she says, looking at the dead baby. "What are those marks on his head?"

"Those are from the instruments the doctor used to get the baby out."

She spends a few moments looking at the dead baby, not making any attempt to pick it up or hold it. She turns to see her daughter still on the delivery table, awake and staring at the ceiling.

Dr. Steve finishes writing notes and orders for the woman. She is carried to a bed in the ward. I attach the donated blood to her IV.

"Rough start today." Dr. Steve gets up from the nurses' desk. "I'll go back to the clinic to see what situations await me there."

"It's so sad to lose a baby. We saved the mother and that feels good. The surgery ward will be a huge benefit to the patients like her," I reassure him.

I see the aide holding Bebé Rémy and coaxing her to drink as I leave the ward.

# Chapter Five

*loiré á Dieu* is the familiar tune of the doxology with the words in French. We are at the Limbé Baptist Church along with hundreds of Haitian worshippers. The front two rows on the left are reserved for the foreign missionaries. We sit shoulder to shoulder. Haitians pack in pews and stand in doorways, at windows, and along the walls; a typical Sunday morning. We walked about a half mile to be here for hours of praying, preaching, and—my favorite—the music. In the choir facing us are many familiar faces of hospital workers. Their faces glow as they praise the Lord in lively song.

I lean over to Rich. "I hope the service ends soon. My stomach is rolling." There are no bathroom facilities here and I am concerned about making the walk back to the compound. An old man bent over a cane shuffles up the middle aisle towards the front of the church. He turns to address the congregation and, with a voice much stronger than his frail body seems capable of, begins to testify to God's grace. He goes on for a few minutes and there are shouts of "Amen" and "Alleluia." More singing. More praying.

As soon as the service is over, I gather my Haitian songbook and recently acquired Haitian New Testament. Haitian Creole is a spoken language, a dialect of French with Spanish, English, and African dialect influences. The words are spelled phonetically. We are so grateful for the Bible to be written in Creole and available to the people.

Many people want to speak with us as we are leaving church. My insides are protesting loudly. Arriving at our house, I spend the remainder of the afternoon between the bathroom and resting in bed. I only hope that I am not suffering with a bacterial infection in my intestines like the last time I was here. That time, I was a victim of salmonella poisoning. Rich brings me chicken noodle soup that was sent to us in a care box from friends in the States.

As evening approaches, I know I have to make rounds in the maternity ward. Rich decides so join me since he knows I'm not feeling well yet. Lisa, a black Labrador that belongs to the compound, walks dutifully with us. She is usually my evening companion when I have night rounds or am summoned during the night. While I am in the ward, she finds a shadowed corner to wait to walk me home.

Rich sits in the rocking chair with Bebé Rémy while I make my visits. The night nurse gives me a brief update before I pass by each bed. I check for fevers and make sure everyone is stable. I am grateful the delivery room is empty for the moment. As the patients are preparing for bed, their family members who are there to care for their needs are bringing in grass mats to lay on the floor near their loved one. The women are not shy about having their chest bare, especially those who are feeding their newborns.

As I get to the second room, I note that Madame Assondier is alone. This is unusual. Typically, there is always someone from her family present. Her mother and mother-in-law are most frequently in attendance. It is rather funny; every time they see me, they say, "There's the mother of the baby." When I realized the baby they meant was Bebé Rémy, I responded with, "No, she's her baby." It has become a regular banter between us.

Now, as I complete a brief examination of her, I ask, "Madame Assondier, where is your family?"

"They're out at the cook area still." She is referring to a cement patio outside the walls of the surgical ward where the families make meals over a small charcoal fire. They use a metal bowl-like contraption with holes in the bottom. It stands about six inches tall on three legs. The Haitian women pull their skirt up between their legs and squat for hours with no seat. I would not last five minutes in that position. I'm not able to balance the large loads on my head like they can, either.

"May I ask you a question?"

Still short of breath when speaking, she simply says, "Yes."

"I've noticed no one in your family visits the baby in the incubator. And no one brings the baby to you. She doesn't even have a name yet. Why is that?"

Looking up at me with sad, tired eyes, she whispers, "They believe the baby is a curse that made me sick."

"No." I consider the enormity of her response. "No. The baby was born early because you had a fever. You were sick. Do you believe she's a curse?"

The slightest shrug of her shoulders. "No."

I hesitate. *How do I proceed here?* There is a keen awareness of evil spirits and curses among the people, especially with the peasant families such as hers. "Madame Assondier, do you believe in Jesus Christ as your personal Savior?"

There is a momentary twinkle in her eyes. "Yes." And with more energy than I've seen from her, she rises up on one arm and leans towards me. "Yes. Yes, I believe. But they don't, or at least I don't believe they do."

"May I pray with you?"

Falling back on the bed, she closes her eyes while I pray for her healing, for the baby, and for the salvation of her family.

Echoing "Amen," she opens her eyes and says, "Please, name my baby. Perhaps that will change the curse into a blessing. You are a White missionary."

I have been asked to name babies before, like the set of twin girls who are named Cherie and Cheriliene, after me.

"The baby's most certainly a blessing. She has survived in spite of many challenges. I will discuss a name with my husband."

A deep sighing breath. She's at peace. The screen door leading into the room opens. Her mother enters with the now-empty charcoal cooker. She places it on the floor by the wall and pulls a folded mat out from under the bed.

"You are taking good care of her. She's better," I say.

"She's still not well, but she is better than she was."

I leave them and walk back through the main ward room. The nurse switches off the lights. Coming around the corner of the nurses' area, I see Rich gently rocking Bebé Rémy and singing to her. "She's a cutie, isn't she?"

Looking at me, he says, "She's adorable. Look at this." Uncovering her thin arm, he holds his small finger next to it to compare. It is the same size. "She's no bigger than a minute."

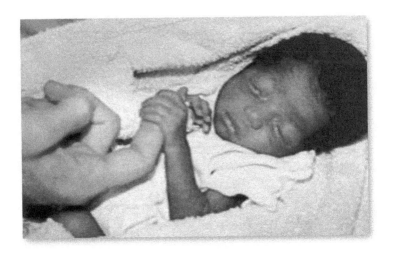

# Chapter Six

"Madame Assondier wants us to name her baby. Any ideas?"

Having explained my interaction with Madame Assondier and her request, we discuss several possibilities. Nothing seems to fit. One possibility is "Rose." That is part of Madame Assondier's given name, "Elirose," and also my middle name.

"Maybe we should choose a biblical name. That will certainly help them see the blessing she is. Although, the baby's condition seems to be worsening since she now has diarrhea, too."

"Which woman of the Bible should we pick? Mary? Elizabeth?"

Laughing, I say, " 'Elizabeth' is too big; it's bigger than she is. I do like the story of Ruth. Maybe we could name her 'Ruth.' "

Rich was contemplative. "Maybe . . ."

"You know, there is one thing that stands out to me about that baby: her eyes. They seem so big in comparison to her frail body. And they always seem so hopeful. They remind me of Georgena's eyes."

Georgena was a dear friend of mine. She was a church member from Painesville First Baptist, my original sending and supporting church. She was a fourth-grade school teacher for nearly thirty years and had helped me study Creole before my first trip to Haiti. She did not know the language—or any foreign language—but she quizzed me with flash cards and vocabulary words to help me. Her friends and family lovingly called her "Little George" because of her short stature. She had a heart of gold.

Georgena was diagnosed with ovarian cancer while I was away for my first trip. She had put up a valiant fight, even flying to Tijuana, Mexico, for an experimental treatment. Rich and I had visited with her prior to making this return trip. I sat by her hospital bed in her dining room, praying for her while she slept. Tears were flowing when I looked up to see her watching me.

"Don't cry for me, Sheri. I know where I am going, and I am ready." There was such a hopeful look in her eyes; they glowed.

Georgena went to her heavenly home two weeks before this tiny baby made her early entrance into the world.

Rich says, "That's what we can name her: 'Little George.' Let's see, would that be 'Ti George'?"

"No, that would be a boy name. *Ette* means 'little' in French. How about 'Georgette'?"

"I like it. Should we give her a middle name, too?"

"Yes, and I like the name 'Ruth' for her middle name. It has great biblical significance: 'Your people shall be my people . . .'"

"Georgette Ruth Rémy."

We pray together for the baby and her mother.

"I will tell Madame Assondier the name we have chosen. I hope she and her family like it."

Later that day, I tell the nurses and aides that Rich and I have been asked to name the baby, and have chosen a fitting name. "I will make a presentation of the baby to her mother."

"What name did you give her?"

"I'll tell Madame Assondier and her family first. You may come and hear my explanation."

Within ten minutes, word spread about the excitement in the back room of the ward. I change the baby's "diaper" and put a fresh shirt on her. As I wrap her tiny, bony frame with wrinkled skin in a receiving blanket, I hope she doesn't have diarrhea while I present her.

Reverently, I cradle the baby in my left arm and make my way through the ward. I arrive at the bedside of Madame Assondier, met by a large and animated crowd of people. Her two mothers were standing at the head of her bed saying, "*Au Dieu,* there she is with her baby."

"She is not my baby. She is *her* baby," I reply, tipping my head toward Madame Assondier. "My husband and I have prayed about a fitting name for your tiny baby." I explain about my friend Georgena who is now in heaven with Jesus and how we called her "Little George" because she was so small. I tell them about the hopeful eyes and her great faith. I share the biblical significance of the book of Ruth. "The name we have chosen for your baby is 'Georgette Ruth.'" And with flourish, I lay the baby next to her mother.

Madame Assondier gently strokes a finger along the cheek of the baby while excited chatter fills the room. Suddenly, Madame Assondier throws her head back and says, "*Au Dieu.*" The room is instantly silenced. "This baby is going to live, and I am going to die."

A pregnant pause ensues as my mind races for a fitting comment. *If anything, this baby won't make it.*

"Don't say that. Look, you're getting better. You can even get up and walk a few steps. You're much better than when your husband carried you down the mountain."

A small voice inside me says, *Pray with them.*

"Please pray with me." I pray for the mother and the baby with a significant name. I also pray, "If there are any here who do not know Jesus as their personal Savior, let them choose Him now. Amen."

I slip away through the crowd and leave the baby with the mother.

# Chapter Seven

"Madame Rich. Madame Rich," whispers Jacque urgently outside my screened window. I awake from my sleep and automatically look at my watch. It's about 5:30 a.m.

"Yes, what is it?"

"Madame Michael sent me to get you. A patient has died in the maternity ward. Come quickly."

I am already wearing my work clothes, accustomed to being summoned at night when I'm on call for emergencies in the maternity ward. Rushing out of the house into the predawn coolness, I have a sense of foreboding. I can hear the wailing before I make it halfway across the open yard near the hospital. There is such a tremendous expression of grief among the Haitian people. My heart turns a somersault as I realize the location of the commotion.

Stepping through the end door of the maternity ward, I am at the bedside of Madame Assondier. Madame Michael sadly shakes her head and hands a stethoscope to me. It is immediately obvious that the mother is not breathing. All her labored efforts of the past are now eerily silent. Her skin is still slightly warm as I place the stethoscope on her chest. The wailing of the family mourners is momentarily silenced as I listen intently for any sign of life from her heart. There is none. I listen for three minutes and it feels like an eternity.

I look at my watch to note the time. "She's gone." A new wave of crying and wailing ensues. No one is asleep in the maternity ward and, likely, not in the medical ward either.

Arrangements are being made and I write a note in her chart. My mind flashes back to her dire prediction two days earlier. Somehow, she knew.

Back home for a few moments, I locate Haitian currency and tuck it in my smock pocket. We are encouraged not to hand out money, but I know there will be a special need in this case.

When I return to the ward, the doctor has been informed of the events and he stops by the ward on his way to the *tonnelle*, the shelter where the triage takes place.

"She didn't have much of a chance. Her heart was too weak," he says.

The family lovingly wraps her body in a sheet. She is placed on a door from a hut that someone has donated. Light rope is used to secure her body to the door to transport her back to the mountain village for burial.

Addressing the grieving family, her husband and the two mothers, I say, "Here is money to help with the cost of taking her home. Please remember, the baby is yours. We'll keep her here until she is a stable weight—five or six pounds. Then, you will be able to take her home. Come to visit and check on her."

Murmurs. More crying.

"I'm so sorry for your loss." My words seem so inadequate.

That was the last time I saw Georgette's mother, her enshrouded body on the door placed in the back of a hired tap-tap truck.

*Lord, now what? What will that baby's chance be now?*

Returning to the delivery area, I pick up a sleepy baby Georgette. "I'm so sorry, baby girl. Your mommy is gone to heaven. We did all we could here, but it was her time to go. If you don't start to grow and get stronger, you will soon be joining her. Hang on, little one. Hang on."

# Chapter Eight

"Doc, can I get your opinion on something?"

Dr. Hodges is finishing breakfast when I stop by. A few volunteers linger at the table. A Haitian staff of three prepares meals for Dr. and Joanna Hodges, the volunteers, and children populating the pediatric ward and the orphan nursery.

"What's on your mind?" Dr. Hodges sits in his customary seat at the head of a long line of tables. It is not uncommon for twelve to twenty people to gather for a meal.

"The baby in the incubator, Georgette. Since her mother passed, she has lost her will to live. She has no appetite. She has diarrhea and has vomited a couple times. What's the most efficient way to rehydrate her?"

"Well," he says, leaning back in his chair and clearing his throat, "you don't have many options. It would be ideal to place a scalp vein IV." He is referring to the practice of inserting an intravenous line in one of the blood vessels on the baby's head.

"Do you think we should do that?"

"She's so dehydrated that finding a suitable vein will be a challenge. Besides, there are other issues to consider." He studies me. "Who will place the IV? Who will manage and care for it? The nurses in the maternity ward are not trained for that—busy with deliveries and their patients. That's not a good choice."

"Should we transfer her to the pediatric ward?"

"That depends on what kind of death you want her to suffer."

I am speechless.

He shrugs. "What I mean is, she has already lived beyond anyone's expectation."

*Except mine.*

He continues. "Dying of dehydration is better than going to the pediatric ward with a hundred sick kids. In her weakened state, she will be exposed to all kinds of germs. And dying from generalized sepsis is harsh."

I find my voice. "But the nurses there have training with babies."

"Yes, the nurses there can place and maintain the scalp vein IV. But they are not accustomed to handling a baby as small as she."

Grasping for hope, I offer another suggestion. "If we can find one small enough, how about a nasogastric tube?"

He shakes his gray head. "You said she's vomiting. If she vomits with an NG tube, she will likely aspirate into her lungs and die from asphyxiation or aspiration pneumonia. Again, dying from infection is a cruel choice."

Clenching my jaw in an attempt to control my frustration, my words are clipped. "I am talking about a way to help her live. Not choosing a way for her to die."

"And you had better be prepared for the reality." Everyone is still as he meets my gaze. "She is going to die. The only questions are when and how."

Tears spring to my eyes. I dig my fingernails into my palms in an effort to hold back the embarrassing emotion. Crying makes me look weak. Being professional translates into keeping emotions on a short leash. Dealing with facts. "I am not ready to give up on her. There is some reason she's still alive. Even with the odds stacked against her."

The doctor sighs. "Suit yourself. You asked for my opinion. You will have to do whatever you think is right. But," he says and leans forward to place his elbows on the table, "be prepared for the consequences."

Heavyhearted, I walk to the hospital. *Lord, what am I to do? What is the best thing for her? Why do I care so much for this one patient?* My questions echo back unanswered.

I detour to the pharmacy supply room. Rich is there.

"I talked with Doc about hydrating Georgette."

"What did he say?"

"To consider the easiest way for her to die."

Rich nods. "He sees so much unnecessary loss. That's what he expects." He studies my face. "What are you going to do?"

"I have no idea. He's right. All the options have undesirable risks." I walk to the storage shelves. "Where did you say you saw some NG tubes?"

"In the last set of shelves. About third shelf from the top."

Going to corner he described, I look through an assortment of NG tubes. Most are adult sizes, 16–18 French. What I really need is an 8 French. My hands are full of different sizes and a few drop to the floor. Bending over to retrieve them, I see a small tube. My heart jumps as I pick it up. Finding the label, I see the size—10 French.

*Is there a way to make this work?*

Shelving the other packages in order of size, I notice a slip of paper between the shelf and the wall. Grabbing it, I realize it is connected to a package. "A 6 French! I found a 6-French NG tube!"

In my excitement, I nearly run over Rich coming around the corner. "What's all the noise about?"

Though Rich serves the mission by working in the pharmacy, he does not have a medical background and does not understand the terminology. I hold up the tube for him to see.

"It's the littlest tube I have ever seen. Imagine finding it here! Now!"

"I thought you said a tube is risky?"

"Is it mere coincidence that tiny tube is here, that I would find it hidden in the shelf?" *Lord, is this a sign? My answer?*

My steps are purposeful as I go to the maternity nurses' station. The younger nurse is there. "Miss Maude, how is Georgette?"

Her eyes are sad. "She is not good, Madame Rich. They can't get her to drink."

At the incubator, I lift the top and reach down to gingerly pick up Georgette's floppy frame. The muscles on the bird-like bones are like wet spaghetti. With great care, I support her head. Her half-closed eyes are sunken in her skull. Her characteristic spark has gone out. She makes the barest whimper.

"I know, baby girl, I know. You are trying so hard." Tears blur my vision and I turn my back to the staff so they don't see my heartbreak. Reaching for the dropper, I try to coax a few life-giving drops through her dry, cracked lips. In slow motion, her small tongue attempts to negotiate the liquid to her throat.

Dr. Steve comes into the delivery area. "I was looking for you. Dr. Hodges told me about your predicament." Over his thick, russet mustache, his blue eyes look from me to Georgette.

I show him the tube I found in the pharmacy. "What should I do?"

"I agree that the tube is risky. She is too weak to swallow to advance the tube down her throat. You risk getting it in the wrong place." He is quiet and I know he is considering options. "A desperate measure would be to surgically put a tube directly in her stomach, but I doubt she is strong enough to survive the procedure. Dehydration is causing her body to shut down."

I turn to Miss Maude. "Has she had any wet diapers?"

"Ma Michelle said she had yellow diarrhea early this morning. If she is dry now, she has not had any more."

I check and the makeshift diaper is disappointingly dry.

Dr. Steve gently rubs his finger over Georgette's severely sunken fontanel and carefully pinches the skin on her forearm. The skin tents and remains wrinkled like a raisin. "Do what you can to get her to take fluid from the dropper. If she doesn't look better after lunch, you have to try the tube."

Dr. Steve leaves and I sink into the rocking chair. Perhaps Georgette is beyond hope and the only thing I can do is hold her so she's not alone when she dies. Many people are in the clinic, waiting to be seen. The longer I stay in this chair, the more my absence puts a strain on the other workers.

Drop after hesitant drop, I squeeze rehydration formula inside her cheek. Maybe it will absorb through the lining of her mouth. With great effort, she manages a swallow.

The aide approaches and asks if she can feed the baby so I can help in the clinic. Reluctantly, I hand the baby to her. "Do what you can, a little at a time. Come and tell me if she vomits or has diarrhea. In a half hour, warm her in the incubator. I will be back at lunchtime."

The morning hours crawl. Although I am seeing patients, my thoughts and silent prayers are focused on the little spark of struggling humanity in the next building. At last, lunchtime arrives and I bolt back to the maternity ward.

"How is she? Did she drink? Has she had a wet diaper?"

The aide just shakes her head.

Peering in the incubator, I see Georgette is sleeping. She's alive. Barely. I let the aide rest and go home for lunch. Rich and I pray for God's will. I plead for guidance to know how to proceed.

Dr. Steve stops by. "I checked on the baby. She's not better. You'll have to attempt the tube. Can you do it?"

"I think so." I am not as concerned about my technical skill as my emotional involvement. I care for the baby more than most would consider professional.

"If you would rather I do it, just say so."

"No. Go home and have your lunch. I'll manage."

On my way to the ward, I stop by the sterilization room to get a syringe. There are no 10 cc syringes so I settle for a 20 cc syringe. Armed with the supplies and my stethoscope, I return to the incubator.

Once again, I carefully lift her from the glass enclosure. Tiny eyelids flutter to reveal the once-bright eyes are rolled back. "No one believes you'll live. And no medical answer can produce the miracle you need, little one."

"Oh Lord," I pray, "why is she here? What purpose can there be for such suffering?" None of my medical training prepared me for this. I chase away thoughts of "if only." It does no good to think about the resources that would be available to Georgette if she were born somewhere else, like the States. "Heavenly Father, I need your help. Right now. What am I supposed to do?"

Holding the baby, I wait for an answer. There are no booming voices, no flashes of light. But a small voice from my heart reaches my head.

*Just love her.*

"But Lord, it'll hurt."

*Just love her.*

Tears flow unchecked and I do not care. "It'll hurt when she goes, Lord. And no matter what the outcome today, she will go. If she dies, she will go. If she lives, she will return to her family and be gone from me."

*Just love her.*

In that moment, I surrender my control. "Okay, God. I will love her. No matter the outcome. I trust You." It feels like a free fall into the arms of a loving Savior. "Love is all I have. Love is all I can give."

I blink away the tears so I can see what I am about to do. *Lord, help me get this in the right place. Don't let anything I do torture her any more than she already has endured.* I remove the tiny NG tube from its package.

Ever so carefully, I support her head and guide the lubricated tip of the tube into her nostril. She grimaces and a weak cry emanates from deep within her. "I'm so sorry, baby. This is what I have to do to help you. Now, swallow." I stroke her throat like I would to get a puppy to take medicine. She starts to gasp and I quickly pull the tube back, afraid it is going into her breathing tube instead of her esophagus.

I am sweating profusely. The aide and Miss Maude come to the table to watch. Advancing the tube, Georgette swallows at the right moment. I advance the tube to the premeasured mark. Attaching the syringe, I inject 1 cc of air as I listen over her belly to make sure the tube is in the correct position. I pull back on the syringe and get a small amount of stomach juice.

Letting out a relieved sigh, I ask Miss Maude to hand me a piece of white medical tape to secure the tube to her nose. Curving the tube up by her temple, I place another piece of tape.

Dr. Steve steps up behind me. I didn't even hear him come in the door. I wipe my tear-stained face on my sleeve.

"I think the tube is in the right place. Will you help me determine the right amount to give her?"

Together, we decide she needs to be hydrated and needs calories for strength. I mix a 50% formula/serum rehydration oral, an electrolyte solution. Initially, Dr. Steve suggests 10 cc of the mixture every hour, to be given slowly. Since she has not had much volume in her stomach, we adjust it to 8 cc at a time. Dr. Steve returns to the bustling clinic.

I give Georgette her first feeding through the tube while the staff watches. I explain several times how important it is to be patient and give her the feeding slowly, for ten or fifteen minutes. I write out an explanation and make a chart of the feeding times. And then, recognizing that it may cause confusion, I put tape around the outside of the syringe at the 8 cc mark.

Tiny arms try to reach up to her face. Georgette is too weak to reach the tube, but I am aware of the need to keep her from pulling it. Taking several small pieces of bandage, we cover her hands and secure it at the wrists. Such a sight. She looks like a boxer with her hands all covered up, and the stark-white tape on her dark face is quite the contrast.

Watching her for another fifteen minutes, she seems to have tolerated the feeding well. I put Georgette in the warm cocoon of the incubator.

"I am going back to the clinic. Do you have any questions?"

They all assure me of their understanding and I leave.

*    *    *    *

Two hours later. . . .

"Madame Rich, Madame Rich! Come quick. Immediately." The aide is on the walk outside where I am consulting patients, shouting through the window.

"What?"

"Madame Rich, Miss Maude sent me to get you. The little baby is dying. Please, come now."

The nurse working with me springs into action and pushes me toward the door.

"I will get someone to see your patients. Go."

My feet propel me toward the back door and I sprint to the orphan nursery door. It is much closer to get to the delivery area than trying to get out the front clinic door. My heart is pounding for more than physical exertion. Dread and fear start to close in as I rush around the corner. In a flash, I take in the scene. Georgette is lying on the table, slowly gasping for breath. It is end-stage breathing. The tube is still in her nose, but the tip that is supposed to be in her stomach is protruding out of her mouth. She is lying in a large puddle of formula solution. It is immediately obvious what has happened. Far too much solution was given much too quickly for her small belly.

I don't think. I act.

"Miss Maude, a delivery kit." I swab the side of her tiny face to clear away the vomit. In one simultaneous move, I have the tube out and I am using the suction bulb from the delivery kit to clear her mouth and nose. The dusky blue color of her lips and the death rattle in her chest are signs the end is imminent.

"The Ambu bag." The aid grabs it from the shelf for me. It has an adult mask on it. There is no way to get any kind of seal when the mask covers her from head to belly. Frantically pumping away anyhow, I look around for anything else that I can use. My eyes fall on the huge green tank that stands near the incubator: it's oxygen. I have never used it. I don't even know if there is anything in it. Pointing at it, I say, "Bring the tank here."

Miss Maude protests. "But, Madame Rich, that is for the delivering women, for an emergency."

"This is an emergency. Now, bring it here." Meanwhile, Georgette's breaths are slower and shallower than before. I place my forefinger on her chest. She has a heartbeat—rapid. Too rapid. Miss Maude and the aide manage to get the tank closer to the table. The tubing and mask have been attached to the tank for an untold period of time. The aide blows dust off the mask.

"This won't fit her either."

"I know, but she needs oxygen. Can you get the tank turned on?" *Please Lord, let there be oxygen in that tank.*

The two women struggle with the regulator and then I hear the air flow come through the tube. Suctioning her mouth and throat one more time, I place the large mask over her face and continue to monitor her heartbeat. Then, I remove the mask altogether and hold the end of the tube in front of her mouth and nose. This goes on for a few minutes. Everyone is silent. *Come on, baby. Come on, baby. Don't die now*, my head is screaming. *Lord, please, if it is your will, don't let her die.*

Miss Maude, who had stepped away for a moment, returns. She breaks the silence when she asks, "Do you want me to go get a box from Rich in the pharmacy?" She is insinuating the dead baby will be ready for the village undertaker to retrieve her body for burial by evening.

Something snaps inside of me. "SHE'S NOT DEAD YET! And you will learn how to take care of her."

Miss Maude, the aide, and several curious onlookers back away from me. I am aware of my burning face and the thought crosses my mind—*they all think I'm crazy.* They have never experienced me like this.

Slowly—very slowly—dusky lips turn pale pink. Her heartbeat slows to a more normal rate and her breathing gets deeper, the rate improving. Her eyes are still rolled back in her head, the white visible through small slits.

I am so totally engrossed in the little life teetering on the edge of this world and the next, I don't realize that Dr. Steve is standing next to me. I am startled when he places his hand on my shoulder. No questions asked. No advice given. I know he is silently praying right along with me.

Moments pass.

"Uuuuuh." A tiny moan comes from Georgette. My heart leaps. "Come on, little one, come back."

I look at Dr. Steve through tear-blurred eyes. "I will not give up on her."

"I know," he says, with his eyes getting moist. "Follow your heart." He squeezes my shoulder and leaves.

*God, you said, "love her." That is all I have. We don't have anything here medically to save her life. Lord, I do love her, and I trust you. Your will be done here.* My silent prayer comes from the deepest place that exists in me.

The aide brings a clean baby blanket and helps me to remove the wet clothing. Swaddling her, I gather baby Georgette in my arms and sit down in the rocker that has been moved next to the oxygen tank. I can do nothing. But I'm determined to be with her, no matter the outcome.

Slowly, I rock her, still holding the oxygen tube in front of her mouth and nose. The rate has been turned down so the tank is not depleted too quickly. I am oblivious to anything happening around me—murmuring staff, the noise outside the clinic door. I no longer feel guilty about not being in the clinic. This is exactly where I am supposed to be.

Word reaches Rich about Georgette's condition. When the clinic day is over, he comes to see us. Unashamedly, I cry as I relate the events to him.

"What are you going to do now?"

"Rock her. Hold her."

"How is she?"

"Better than she was a couple hours ago. Still critical. Still dehydrated. But breathing better. I hope she didn't aspirate into her lungs. She has a little rattle sound in there."

"Will you be able to come home to eat?"

"I am not leaving her. They'll kill her."

"You have to eat. You have to keep your strength up, too."

"I'm staying. I'll drink water, pray, and fast."

"All right. If you're sure. I'll bring you water." He caresses her cheek and leans down and gives her a kiss on her forehead. "Hang in there, pumpkin."

A little while later, Dr. Hodges comes through the ward making the night rounds for Cheryl. She returned from her unannounced hiatus several days after Madame Assondier passed. I continued the special attention to Georgette while turning the remainder of the maternity responsibilities to her.

Now, Dr. Hodges stands in front of the rocking chair. "I understand you had a close call with her today."

I recount the events to him, keeping my emotions in check. *What if he thinks I misused the oxygen resource?* He doesn't mention the oxygen at all.

"You'll still need to get her hydrated."

"I know. I'm considering putting the tube down again and managing it myself."

"That's quite a commitment."

"I believe she's worth every effort."

"Carry on, then. I'll check on the patients in the ward."

He leaves and I resume my rocking. Her color is improved, so I decide to remove the oxygen and see what happens. I turn off the tank, hoping I won't need it again, and settle back in the chair with an extra blanket to keep her warm.

Rich returns with a large container of citrus juice and ice water. With coaxing, he convinces me to leave the ward for a few minutes so I can use the restroom. He takes my place in the rocking chair, snuggling Georgette close. It feels good to stretch my legs and walk back to the house.

I return wearing a different outfit. I know I'll be here through the night, if needed. Rich protests to my plan. But he knows I've made my mind up and won't be persuaded otherwise. I can be stubborn; I prefer to think of it as determined.

While Rich watches, I successfully place the NG tube again. Georgette's eyes flutter in response. I don't put anything through the tube right away. I want to make sure her breathing remains stable. Breathe in. Breathe out. My vigil continues as I stare through the glass top of the incubator. Reluctantly, Rich leaves.

Madame Tony is on the night shift. "How's that baby doing now? Miss Maude told me she's near dead."

"She is in God's hands. His will be done."

Choosing to use the rehydration solution alone for the first feeding, I slowly infuse it. Holding her, I give her 1 cc at a time, praying continuously. Hourly, I warm her in the incubator. *Will the daylight ever come?*

# Chapter Nine

S unken, but brighter, eyes fix themselves on my face. I imagine she is saying "thank you." Through the routine of the night, Georgette and I have bonded on an inexplicably deep level. And together, I'm aware we're being held in God's arms.

The ward begins to come alive for the day. Cheryl stops to see us as she's making the morning rounds. "How is she?"

Georgette is snuggled in my arms. "She's better than she was. But then, anything's better than yesterday. She finally had a wet diaper. I didn't know I could get so excited to change a diaper."

Cheryl peers in to the blanket. "Her hydration is still terrible. I am glad you are the one taking care of her. I still don't see she has much chance." She turns to answer a question for the nurse. *I'm glad to be the one taking care of Georgette, too.*

One by one, we get visits from Rich, Dr. Steve, Dr. Hodges, and other volunteers and staff. In their eyes, I read sadness. It may be for the hopelessness they still see in her condition. Or, perhaps, it's for my dogged determination in spite of what seems to be hopeless.

"I'll be staying here with the baby and I'm not coming to the clinic this morning." There is no feeling of guilt or obligation. I'm at peace knowing this is where I'm meant to be right now.

"I suspected such." Dr. Hodges leaves to begin the half-day clinic.

Through the morning and into the afternoon, I do not relinquish my post. I've switched the formula back to the 50/50 solution. She tolerates the slow feedings well. Thankfully, she hasn't vomited.

Late in the afternoon, Rich excitedly hurries to the delivery area and is smiling. "I got the mail and boxes that came from Agape." Agape Flights is our connection to the rest of the world. They make weekly flights to bring us our mail and supplies. A driver from the mission travels to Cap-Haïtien on Saturday afternoons to retrieve the items from the customs agents.

"I was going through surgery supplies that came from the States. I found something that seemed out of place with the other items. I wonder if it's what you need for her." He extends his hand and I know, in that instant, that God has provided. Pure gold holds no value to what someone chose to add to a box of "throw-away" items. There, in his hand, is one sterile-sealed preemie bottle nipple.

Hope balloons in my heart. There could be a note attached from God saying "It's okay. I'm in control." Happy tears and a grin redefine my face.

Through the remainder of the afternoon and evening, our routine becomes offer bottle, pray, feed through tube, hold and rock, pray, warm in incubator, check diaper, and repeat. She's still so weak and doesn't seem to know what to do with the bottle. Rich takes my place for a short while.

"You must eat and sleep," he says.

"How can I trust anyone else to take care of her? She still isn't drinking from the bottle and the staff isn't capable of managing the feeding tube." I'm not able to stay away.

# Chapter Ten

My relentless vigil continues. I sit in the rocking chair, holding sleeping Georgette. The feeding tube is still the best way to get life-saving liquid in her body. Earlier, her eyes were open and clearer than they have been for days.

I struggle to keep my eyes open. My head begins to bob and I snap it back up, willing myself not to give in to the exhaustion washing over me. It's quiet in the ward this morning.

During the night, there were two deliveries which I did for the nurses since I was there anyhow. They were uncomplicated deliveries and Georgette waited for me in the incubator while I helped to bring miraculous new life into the world. A new birth is such an incredible experience. One person comes in and two lives leave the delivery area. *It is a beautiful human life event and one that should never be taken for granted*. As I hold a newborn in my hands, I am grateful for the talent given to me and the enormous potential each new life holds within it.

Heavy eyes.

The next thing I am aware of is Haitians singing worship music. Although I cannot see them from where I am sitting, their blend of voices touches me deeply. They sing with joy and assurance at the near end of the maternity ward. I hear the patients clapping along and shouting with praise. After a long prayer, the group moves on to the medical ward.

"Church must be over." I'm carrying on a conversation with Little Miss Bright Eyes—Georgette. She squirms in my arms and her left-covered hand pops out of the blanket. In my near-delirious state, I imagine she is raising her arm in praise.

Rich checks on us. He ate lunch with one of the other missionary families and brought a plate of food for me.

"I'll trade you. You take the food and I can hold her for a little bit."

My mouth begins to salivate as I take the plate and uncover it. There is cooked rabbit, which tastes like chicken. The mission raises the rabbits for food and the blood is used for the agar plates in the laboratory. There is also fried plantain, beans and rice, and fresh pineapple slices. Beans and rice are not my favorite but they are a staple of the Haitian diet, and at this moment, they are delicious. I didn't realize how hungry I was. He also brought a large cold cup of sweetened citrus juice made from the oranges, grapefruit, and small lemons called citron.

"You looked wiped out." He is gently rocking Georgette and stroking her head with one finger.

"I'm getting there."

"Can I try to feed her with the bottle?"

"Sure. After all, you found the nipple. She still doesn't seem to know what to do with it and only plays with it. I have noticed that she likes to put her hand to her mouth. If her hands weren't covered, she would probably be sucking her thumb. I wonder if she did that in utero."

"It does make you wonder what she experienced while she was being carried. I mean, I wonder if she heard the voodoo drums and things like that."

"I would assume so."

"Do you think she'll make it?"

"I never thought she wouldn't, but it was close on Friday afternoon. She's a long way from being out of the woods, but I have a sense of peace about it. God is in control. I'll accept the outcome, even if it's difficult."

The food and the visit revive me. Rich gives her back to me and promises to check on us again in a couple of hours. He plans to answer letters that came in the mail yesterday.

After a warming session in the incubator, I happily change a wet diaper and resume my routine. Although she is so tiny, it feels so natural to hold her in my left arm and feed her with my right hand.

"I wish you could get the hang of sucking on this bottle." Her tongue plays with the nipple and she takes a few swallows. "See how easy that is?"

Out of the corner of my eye, I see Madame Rafael looking at us. She has a half smile and shakes her head. My coaxing and chatter continues.

Rich returns a few hours later, as promised.

"I insist. Come home and sleep."

My resolve is weakening. My thinking is fuzzy.

Madame Rafael quietly slips up near us. "Madame Rich, I can see what you're doing is making a difference for that little baby. I see love is making her better. If you'll trust me, I will take care of her for you. I've watched you give the formula in the tube. Slowly. You are patient with her and the bottle. I can do that. You need to go home now. Go home with Rich."

"But—"

"Madame Rich, you will be able to help her better after you sleep." She reaches out and gently takes the baby from my arms.

I am too exhausted to protest any more. *I said you are in control, God. I guess I should let you be.* Rich helps me up out of the rocking chair that has been my home for the last three days.

"Remember to warm her in the incubator every hour or so, and don't change the temperature setting. And keep track of how many wet diapers—"

"I know, Madame Rich. I'll take care of her like she was my own."

Not able to resist, my eyes flood and a waterfall cascades over my cheeks. "Thank you, Madame Rafael. I do trust you with her. You are a great friend and an excellent nurse. Thank you."

Gently, Rich guides me out of the delivery area. I look back one last time and wonder if it will be the last time I see baby Georgette alive. Madame Rafael has her snuggled in her arm and is smiling down at her.

I lean on Rich and we slowly walk home. In my exhaustion, I don't even consider the fact that Madame Rafael will be finished with her shift in an hour. *Some food and a shower would be good.* Rich finds me a moment later, sound asleep sprawled on the bed.

# Chapter Eleven

I awake with a start and attempt to get my bearings. I have been dreaming and am disoriented for a moment.

Rich sits on the edge of the bed with his cup of coffee. "Good morning, sleepy head."

"Oh my. What day is this? What time is it?"

"It's Monday and about time for me to go to the pharmacy. How do you feel?"

"My head hurts and I think I'm hungry." Suddenly, my brain clicks into gear. "Wait. Have you heard anything about the baby? Did anybody come to get me while I was asleep?" I jump up out of bed still wearing yesterday's clothes.

Rich steadies me as I wobble from the sudden change in position and adrenaline rush. "No. No one has come to get you and I haven't heard anything yet. I'm sure they would've come to get you if they needed you."

"I'm going to take a quick shower and go back over there."

"I made oatmeal with brown sugar and raisins for you. Eat before you go." He gives me a long hug and leaves.

Twenty-five minutes later, I am out the door rushing to the hospital. My hair is still wet and my stomach full. A fresh dress and clean smock feel cool against my skin. With conscious effort, I slow my steps by the main office door. I hear a commotion from up ahead. My heart flops in my chest. It can be difficult to determine if the racket the Haitians are making is happy or sad, like the death wailing. I'm one step away when the maternity ward door flings open from inside. *Oh no, she died. And no one came to get me.*

"Madame Rich!" shouts the aide who saw my approach. She grabs my wrist and pulls me up into the ward. I'm bewildered and I uncharacteristically assume the worst.

I notice there's a crowd of ten or more hospital workers and others. They are indeed making a lot of noise. I search their faces for emotion—happy. They're dancing. I'm pushed through the crowd. The bodies part. The center of attention is Madame Rafael in the rocking chair. She's beaming. And in her arms is baby Georgette, sucking away on a bottle like there's no tomorrow.

"Madame Rafael?"

"Yes, Madame Rich."

I get down on my knees in front of her to see the baby. Georgette's eyes turn to me, but her industrious feeding is not the least interrupted. I notice something: the tube is missing.

"Who took out the tube? Did one of the doctors? I wasn't going to take it out until we knew she could drink."

"She took it out."

"What? What do you mean?"

"I stayed the night with her. A pregnant woman needed to be delivered while Madame Tony took care of a patient in the ward. I put the baby in the incubator while I worked. When I turned around, she had her hands unwrapped. The tube was in her hand, not her nose. I guess she was done with it." There is laughter all around me.

Standing up, I look around at the faces of those who are seeing this miracle of life.

"I feel like praying. Will you all join me?" I pour out my gratitude to God for saving this little baby's life for His purposes, to show His strength when we had nothing left, and for His perfect will. I hear audible "Amens" all around me.

When I finish, Madame Rafael lifts Georgette to me. Seeing the wet mark on her smock, I know a diaper change is needed. The workers leave to undertake their tasks for the day.

Miss Maude, who had been so ready to bury the baby on Friday, is at my right side as I change the diaper and coo at Georgette. She says, "Someday, this little baby will be a big testimony for God."

"Yes, she will. She already is."

# Chapter Twelve

The days have flown. I'm busy preparing the surgical ward for the first team to arrive from the States in November. That requires the facilities to be ready, as well as equipment, staff, and patients. With the diligent help of the Haitian staff, we're making great progress. Two medical residents have volunteered to help in the clinic for the next two months, which eases the workload for everyone.

Georgette is the bright spot in my day.

Her weight has fluctuated but, generally, she's gaining about a half ounce per day. Her hydration status has improved. Her skin is less wrinkled, so she no longer resembles a raisin. She didn't develop aspiration pneumonia as I feared might happen from her vomiting the feeding tube. The diarrhea is still a periodic problem, so we stopped the daily antibiotics to see if that helps.

Now, the nurses and the aides in maternity have great pride and interest in helping with Georgette's care. The story gets retold of how close to death this tiny baby came and how God saved her. Rich and I take her to our house for short visits and a warm bath, which she seems to enjoy.

Her father and two grandmothers came to see her a few days after we sent word for them to visit their baby. They entered the delivery area while I was still fussing with her flowered dress. Her first floor-length dress. All clothes are too big for her. Seeing us, one grandma says, "Oh Lord, there she is with her baby."

Smiling, I respond, "She's your baby now. She still needs to gain weight, but now I'm certain she'll get up to five or six pounds and go home with you."

The other grandmother hands me a basket with coconut, pineapple, and mango. "This is for you."

"Thank you. You didn't need to bring a gift. Do you want to hold her?"

Hesitantly, Georgette's maternal grandmother takes her from me. She gently bounces the baby in her arms. There is rapid conversation between the family members, not all of which I understand. I hear one say how much she resembles her father, who is standing stoically and quietly behind the women.

I address Assondier. "Will you be ready for the baby to come home in a month or six weeks?"

He diverts his eyes and doesn't answer. Instead, he fidgets with the straw hat in his hand. Eyes tinged with sadness meet mine. He motions his head to the side and steps away from the women. I join him around the corner.

In a hushed whisper, he tells me, "I won't be able to take that baby home. I have no wife to care for her. I am a farmer in the field from before sunrise until after the sun goes down."

"What about them?" I nod in the direction of the women.

"They can't take care of a baby that small, either. My other daughter is three-and-a-half years old and was hospitalized in pediatrics two weeks ago. Malnutrition. And her," he says, gesturing to his mother-in-law. "She is not good in the head and lives down the mountain."

"Is there any other family to help you?"

"No, Madame. Our plan was to leave her for the orphan nursery here. That'll be best for her. We can't take care of her."

"I understand." *Such a valiant fight for life to be destined for an orphanage?* We move toward the women. The other grandmother is holding the baby. It is the first time I've seen them hold Georgette since her birth. The grandmother hands the baby to Assondier. He looks uncomfortable. Her tiny body is so frail in his field-hardened hands. After a few short moments, he gives Georgette to me.

Their visit is brief. I unpack the basket of their gifts and hold the pineapple to my nose with my free hand. I close my eyes and inhale deeply. I almost taste the sweetness. "My husband and I love these fruits. Thank you." It cost them to make the trip—the transportation, the gift, and the emotions of returning to where they lost Georgette's mother and, now, the baby. I'm still hopeful that they will choose to take her home one day.

*    *    *    *

A few nights later, we take Georgette to our house for a warm bath. First, we heat a kettle of water on the propane gas stove. The hospital has created a safe well-water system for the town of Limbé and we have access to the fresh water in the homes on the mission compound, but it is only cold water. Rich adds the warmed water to the square, yellow plastic tub—the kind used for sponge baths in a stateside hospital while I remove her over-sized clothes and "diaper". Gently, I lower her into the warm, bubbly water and together we give her a bath. As I lift her out and we dry her off, I hold her in my hands and Rich snaps a picture. Her big, bright eyes are looking up at me and she has her left arm raised in the air.

"Look at her! This is her victory-over-death pose."

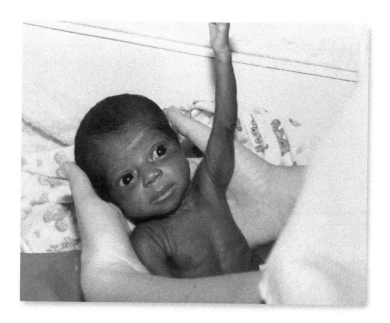

"She sure is a little fighter," says Rich. "Show me how you make that bandage work for a diaper."

I fold the four-inch-wide strip of torn white bedsheet into several layers and use a thin strip to hold the top of it around her miniature waist.

"You are pretty good at that."

"I suppose. I wonder if the volunteers in the States had any idea how their bedsheets would be used—

Suddenly, we hear loud gunfire.

Quickly moving to the hallway where there are block walls on both sides, the three of us huddle on the floor together. I am frightened and bewildered. In hushed voices, we try to determine what the shooting means.

A few weeks ago, the hospital was attacked by a militant group of young ruffians. It was their attempt to "deshooké" or take over the hospital. Bottles and rocks were thrown at the hospital walls. Thankfully, hospital staff and the workers were able to convince them to leave the hospital alone as it serves their many families. A succession of different leaders has attempted to control this island nation since the overthrow of Jean-Claude Duvalier in 1986. The unrest is pervasive.

Now, we don't know who is shooting or why. Even if we are not a target, only having screens to cover our windows means a stray bullet could be deadly.

"Should we call someone else?" There's a phone on the front screened porch. It's only connected to the other houses on the mission compound. Unsure of our risks, we pray for safety together. Georgette starts to cry, so I scramble across the floor to the kitchen to get a bottle.

There is a momentary lull in the gunfire. We can hear yelling from the dirt village road adjacent to the mission compound. A wall surrounds most of the mission. Rich is feeding Georgette and I move below the window line to the phone. Three different numbers ring before I get an answer. It's Dr. Steve. Their house is past ours and close to the main paved road that connects Port-au-Prince in the south to Cap-Haïtien in the north.

"We don't know who or why they are shooting. Stay in your house until we get an all clear."

"We brought Georgette to the house for a bath tonight. How dangerous will it be for her to not be in the incubator?"

"Keep her wrapped up and warm. Your body heat will help."

Another round of gunfire begins, and I quickly return to Rich and Georgette.

"Dr. Steve doesn't know the reason for the gunfire. He wants us to keep the baby warm and wait for instructions."

Rich arranges couch cushions on the floor. I curl up with Georgette next to me and wait.

After an hour or so, we begin to hear a different noise. *Is that a tank rumble?* Gunfire begins to lessen. There is another rumble, louder this time. As the first drops of rain begin to fall on our corrugated steel roof, I realize the rumble is actually thunder.

"Praise the Lord." Haitians do not like to be out in the rain. "This is God's way of protecting us."

The hesitant drops turn into a full downpour. All gunfire ceases. *How many injured will we receive at the hospital as a result of this event?*

After a soaking rain for about thirty minutes, the phone rings. It's Barbara Hodges. She tells me, "It's all clear. The gunfire was a group of men shooting into the air in protest of the change in the militia. We're not in danger, but I'd remain inside for a while longer."

"We have Georgette at our house and need to get her back to the incubator."

"I'll send one of the men to escort you to the hospital."

About an hour later, I hear Jacques. "Madame Rich? I'll go with you to the hospital and back. Are you ready?"

Gathering up the sleeping Georgette and an umbrella, since there is still a light rain falling, I step out into the cool, damp darkness. The walk to the maternity ward and back is without incident. Only one person with a gunshot injury to the arm was being seen by Dr. Hodges in the clinic.

It's a good thing our family back home doesn't know all that happens here. They'd worry more than they already do. It seems only bad news can make it to the media in the States.

# Chapter Thirteen

'm sorting supplies in the surgery depot when Jacques finds me. "Madame Rich, Miss Cheryl sent me to find you. She wants you to come to the delivery area."

My heart skips a beat. Georgette has been doing so well drinking from the bottle and slowly, but surely, gaining weight. Rich and I spend as much time with her as we can. We take her home for a warm bath every couple of days. One of the short-term volunteers has crocheted Georgette a melon-orange stocking cap to preserve her heat. In a care box from our supporting church, we've received newborn size disposable diapers, that are still too large for her. They also sent a preemie-size pacifier, which we have tried to use a few times.

Taking the back walkway from the surgery unit to the orphan nursery and maternity ward, I find Cheryl talking with Dr. Steve. Behind them, I see the nurses are taking care of a couple of newborns. There is one woman on a delivery table, and she looks exhausted. I recognize her as one of the pregnant patients admitted for bed rest because she was having labor signs with twins.

Dr. Steve is sweating through his shirt and light blue smock. "We have a situation. This woman delivered her twins prematurely. The boy babies are small. Three pounds, five ounces and three pounds, eight ounces. We need to put them in the incubator."

Cheryl says, "Maybe we can move Georgette to the crib in the corner. The nurses could still keep an eye on her and feed her there."

Looking at Georgette's chart, Dr. Steve smiles, "She's up to three pounds and fifteen ounces. She's bigger than someone else, finally. But she's still quite small. What do you think we should do?"

"A concern of mine is the amount of care three little babies will require by the staff—especially at night. They have a difficult time keeping up with Georgette." I look at the wooden crib in the corner. It seems massive for such a little baby. "She's still too small to move to the orphan nursery and I certainly don't think it's wise to move her to the pediatric ward. Too many sick children to be exposed to while she's still so little."

"I agree completely." Dr. Steve's forehead is creased with concern. "Has Georgette's family been back to see her?"

"They only came one time, when we sent for them. The father doesn't think they can take care of her. Let me talk with Rich. Maybe we can come up with a solution. Meanwhile, I will put Georgette in the corner crib." I go to the incubator and lift Georgette. "Half-Pint, you are being evicted because there are smaller babies. You get to move to a big-girl crib."

After explaining our plan to the staff, the aide places a sheet over the crib pad for Georgette. I wrap an extra towel around Georgette to maintain her heat.

On my way to the pharmacy to talk with Rich, I pass Jacques speaking with Madame Rafael. "Madame Rich?"

"Yes, Jacques?"

"Last week, Leon and I were going through the depot in the upstairs of Texas. We saw something that looks like an incubator—or parts of one, anyhow."

"Texas" is the name of a building that has rooms for volunteers, storage upstairs, and an open area below where the carpenters plane wood for the woodshop. There are many items that the carpenters make for the hospital, including cribs, tables, chairs, and doors.

"Are you sure?" I ask.

"I'm not sure because there's a lot in the storage room. Doctor has many artifacts from the Puerto Real archeological dig and items people bring him for the museum."

"Thank you, Jacques. I'll speak with Doctor."

I find Rich at the desk in the back of the pharmacy, checking lists of supplies.

"We are having such a difficult time getting IV solution from the supply company in Port-au-Prince. All the political unrest has closed the main road and the trucks can't get through. I don't know what we'll do if there is more than one or two patients who need it today. Barbara's checking if the Catholic hospital at the other side of Limbé has any they can lend us until the truck arrives. But I'm sure you didn't come to hear my problems. What's wrong? You look troubled."

"Georgette is being evicted from the incubator. Twin newborn boys weighing less than her need it. We're trying to decide what to do with Georgette. Right now, she's in the crib in the corner of the delivery room. I worry the staff, especially at night, have so many responsibilities that she will be overlooked. I don't want her to regress."

"That's too bad. How small are the twins?"

"They weigh three-five and three-eight. They're in the incubator together right now. Jacques told me about parts for an incubator he saw in the storage room of Texas. I'm going to find out from Doctor if that's possible. Or maybe we could make a type of incubator to keep her warm."

"That doesn't take care of the problem of not enough staff attention, even if there's another incubator."

"You're right. Maybe I should talk to Joanna about adding another aide for the night shift until the little babies get bigger. I'll go check with her and speak with Doctor at lunchtime."

As I approach the main office door, I can hear Joanna speaking emphatically to a young Haitian man. "We need those supplies from CARE so we can feed the children in pediatrics and provide food for the hundreds of diabetics and others who rely on those rations."

"Madame Doctor, we are doing everything we can to get those supplies, but the road—"

"I know. All this unrest and uncertainty is making everything difficult. When do you think we can get them? The storage depot with the rations is nearly empty."

"I hope by the end of the week. I can't make any promises."

"Well, then we'll make do as best we can."

The young Haitian man wearing a tan uniform walks past me. I am not sure what type of official he is. He's in a hurry.

"All this unrest is hurting a lot of people." Joanna's looking down at papers as I approach the counter.

"Hi, Joanna. May I interrupt you?"

"What can I do for you? We are behind in receiving the CARE rations." Her bright blue eyes peer through glasses at me. She's tense and frustrated.

"I'm sorry to hear that. Rich is having a similar problem in the pharmacy. The supply truck with the IV fluid cannot get through and we have all but depleted our stock. But that's not why I'm here."

I explain the situation with the incubator and the newborn twins. "Is there a way we can add another aide to the night shift to be sure the babies are getting the attention they all need?"

"Well, it is not easy to find women to leave their family at night if they are married, or a single woman to work the night shift. I have a hard time getting the people we have right now."

"Also, Jacques mentioned there may be an incubator or incubator parts in the Texas storage depot. Do you know anything about that?"

"Now that you mention it, I do believe an incubator was sent a while ago, but it either does not work or is missing parts. I didn't think we still had it."

"Would it be possible to find out if it's there? I plan to talk to Doctor about it."

"He would know best what is in that storage depot. It has many items for our museum across the main road and he keeps track of that. The archeology dig was a good hobby for him. With all the unrest, he doesn't feel like it's safe to travel to the site. People are always bringing him pieces of pottery and other things they find."

"I'll check with Doctor."

"Yes, that's what you should do. I don't think we'll be able to add a worker to maternity on nights. The pediatric ward is so busy now, too. I can't move anyone to maternity."

A little while later, the clinic closes for lunch. Dr. Hodges employs a swift and purposeful stride away from the clinic door. A persistent man, wearing a tattered T-shirt and pants with large holes, pursues him. "Doctor, my son is very sick with fever. He needs a ticket to be seen."

"We've already given tickets for patients to be seen this morning."

"But please, Doctor. We couldn't get here any sooner with the roadblocks."

Stopping to listen to the man's story, Doctor gets a paper ticket from his front smock pocket, writes on it, and hands it to the man. "Bring him to the clinic at 2:00 when we return. I'll see him."

Turning and continuing along the walk, others try to stop him also. Holding up his hand, he says, "We'll be back in a little while."

Determined to catch him before lunch, I cut a diagonal path to meet him a bit closer to his house. "Doctor."

He continues up the few steps to the porch, then stops, turns, and lets out his piercing whistle. This is meant to let all the volunteers know it's mealtime.

Looking at me, he says, "I had to get the whistle done. How are things coming for the surgery ward? We have a surgical team ready to come next month. Will you be ready?"

"I hope so. We still need a lot of equipment and I'm starting to train the staff for the post-operative care and sterile technique."

"Quite an undertaking."

"It is. It'll be wonderful when we're able to provide surgical service to people. I wanted to ask you about an incubator or incubator parts that Jacques thought he saw in the Texas depot. We have a couple small twins in the incubator right now."

"What did you do with the little baby you were watching so closely?"

"We had to move her out to make room for the newborn twins. That's why I wondered if there's another one or if we can make one for her."

"Make one?" He looks at me to see if I'm joking. "I do recall parts of one in that depot."

"May I have permission to have Jacques check on it?"

"Of course. But if I remember, it didn't work and there was no way to get more parts for it. You are welcome to whatever you find. I'm going to eat now."

Elated, I let Rich know I'll be late for lunch and go to find Jacques. He's eating a mango that he peeled with his teeth.

"Doctor says we can look for the incubator in the Texas depot. Can you and Leon see what is there and bring it down to the shop?"

"Yes, Madame Rich. We'll do it this afternoon."

"It'll be important to check as soon as possible. Remember the baby I took back to maternity when you escorted me? She needs it."

Over lunch, Rich and I talk more about the situation for Georgette. "What if we were to bring her here for the nights and have the aides take care of her during the day?"

"How will we keep her warm?"

"Maybe the incubator will work or at least be able to keep her body heat contained."

"Let's see what happens this afternoon. It'd be good to bring her here, but do you think we'd get much sleep?"

"Hopefully she will continue to grow and won't need the incubator or as much care through the night. Right now, she needs to be fed every three hours. We can take turns."

After the midday break, Jacques finds me. "We brought down the parts of an incubator. It doesn't work. David Hodges is looking at it in the shop."

David is one of Doctor and Joanna Hodges' grown sons. He is about six foot one with long black hair. He and his wife, Emily, have a baby boy. I rush to the shop, seeing David looking inside a panel of wires with a flashlight. I ask, "What do you think?"

"It doesn't work."

"Is there a way to make it work?" I persist.

"There are burned wires. I'll have the guys see what they can do."

"Thank you. There's a baby who'll thank you, too."

"No promise."

Stopping by maternity to check on Georgette, I find Rich feeding her a bottle. "You look like a natural."

Smiling, he says, "I thought I'd have a few minutes before I return to the pharmacy. The twins are cute. It seems funny to see the two of them in one incubator."

"David and the shop men are working on the other incubator. He doesn't know if it can be fixed. It's a lot newer model than this old thing. It has a plastic box-like top with the arm holes. It sits on a big metal base and is more sophisticated than this one. I hope they get it functioning."

"The crib seems so big for Georgette. It'd be good if we had a small cradle for her."

"She'd fit in a basket. Maybe we should use that one I have at the house."

"That's an idea."

"I have to get back to the surgery ward. I have a lot of sutures to sort and supplies to get into the cabinets in the operating rooms. I'll get the basket a little later."

Madame Abner is waiting for me when I return to the surgery ward. She is unsure about the proper instruments to place in the large lap pack, the set of instruments for major abdominal surgery. "Madame Rich, we do not have any of the large retractors to put in this set. What will we do?"

"I'll look again in the storage depot to see if I can find something that will work as a retractor. Otherwise, maybe the men in the shop can make one." *The littlest things are frustrating.*

"You haven't forgotten my invitation to come visit my home, have you?"

"No, I have not forgotten. I promise. Rich and I will come."

Later, Jacques finds me and has a big smile. "They have the incubator working. But it may still have an electrical issue."

"Is it safe? Can it be used?"

"David says yes. Where do you want us to take it?"

Making a decision on the spot, "Please take it to our house. Madame Edmond is there and can show you a place in the dining room to place it." I hope Rich is good with this.

At the end of the workday, I go to maternity. Cheryl is coming in to check on everyone before dinner. "We are going to take Georgette home with us for the night. The guys fixed an incubator and it's at our house. Joanna didn't think it possible to get an extra aide for the nights here."

"That will be a lot of work for you and Rich."

"It's for a short while. Soon she will be big enough for the orphan nursery. And, who knows, her family may reconsider when they see how well she is doing then."

I write a chart note. *Taking her home since incubator is needed for two other babies. Slight fever: 100°F this p.m. » rhyme.* Rhyme, pronounced "ream," means she has a runny nose.

With a bottle, a can of formula, and Georgette wrapped up in a blanket, I stop by the pharmacy office. Rich stops counting charts with one of the other volunteers. "Who do have you there?"

"Meet our new roommate. The incubator has been taken to our house and supposedly works, although it may still have electrical issue. It will be better than having her in that crib. Are you good with this, for a little while?"

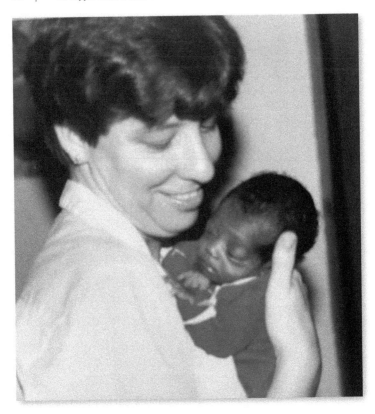

He looks up at me over his glasses with a smile on his face. "Sure."

At our house, Madame Edmond is getting our supper on the table when I enter with Georgette.

"Madame Rich, the men brought a machine for the baby. I had them put it here." She takes the baby from me as I look over the incubator. There are more knobs and lights and the plastic top lifts from the base. Plugging it in, a shrill beep comes from the machine. I yank the cord out of the socket.

"I wonder what that's all about."

Madame Edmond is entranced with the tiny baby she is holding in her arms. She is cooing and clucking, and Georgette is looking up at her glasses and salt-and-peppered hair.

"Jacques said to call David if there's a problem."

I call David on the compound phone and tell him what happened when I plugged the incubator in to the wall. He agrees to come over and see what can be done.

Meanwhile, I inspect the infant chair that Nancy, Dr. Steve's wife, brought by the house earlier. It is a bright blue mesh material over a bent, thin metal frame. It has a slight bounce to it when I push down on the top of the chair. I also look over the woven basket that has handles on either end. It is about two feet long and one foot wide. Both seem perfect for Georgette. I hold her while Madame Edmond arranges blankets in the infant seat. With her little melon-colored knit cap and all the blankets, we can barely see her tiny face when she's in the seat.

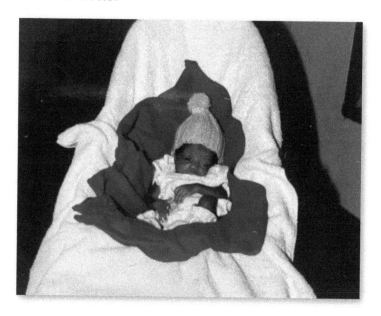

David enters and goes straight to the incubator and pulls it away from the wall. Plugging it in, the shrill sound hurts our ears. Disconnecting it, he produces a screwdriver and removes a back panel. "I think it is a grounding problem."

After several more trials, he decides to remove the third prong on the plug. Finally, the sound is gone.

"You'll have to be careful touching the metal base with both hands if you are in bare feet on the concrete floor. You may get a light shock."

"Are you kidding? What's the risk for the baby?"

"The baby will not feel any shock. You may because *you* are the ground. If you have shoes on or if you only touch one hand to the metal, you'll be okay. The warmer works well and there is an alarm if it gets too warm or too cold." He demonstrates how to adjust the dials and settings.

Rich arrives in time for instructions on the incubator. "It's a good thing the maternity aides aren't responsible for this. You had enough challenge with them using the simple one they have."

Madame Edmond has been quietly standing in the door to the kitchen. "You should eat. Your food is getting cold."

"And it's one of our favorites. Shrimp Creole over rice and sliced pineapple," I add.

Placing Georgette in the incubator, our evening commences.

# Chapter Fourteen

"The staff members I am working with for the surgery ward are fast learners. We covered sterile dressing changes and how to scrub and gown for surgery. I'm pleased with how everything's coming together," I say to Rich from across the table.

"I wonder when the exam table our church sent is going to arrive," Rich ponders aloud.

The family practice I left in the States donated an extra exam table they no longer needed. It's an extremely heavy metal piece with drawers, an adjustable vinyl top, and stirrups. Friends drove it to Florida weeks ago for it to be placed in a shipping container with other donated equipment.

"I hope it all arrives soon. We only have a month until the first surgical team comes."

Rich and I are eating lunch at home. Madame Edmond made our traditional Thursday lunch, pumpkin soup. Haitian pumpkin is a hard-shelled, green-and-white-colored squash. The flesh of the pumpkin is cooked down to make a creamy, light-orange soup. There are a few pieces of meat and carrots. I think the meat is beef, but it could be *cabrite*, otherwise known as goat. The Haitians and few missionaries, who have the stomach for it, add a few drops of *pima*, an intense hot pepper sauce. I made a mistake once and licked a spoon that had been used to get the pepper juice from the jar. It felt like layers were removed from my mouth.

We enjoy our soup and are anticipating the fresh, hot cinnamon tea ring which has that sweet, homey aroma wafting from the kitchen. Suddenly, Rich says, "I think she's supposed to be ours."

"What? Who?"

"Georgette. I think she is supposed to be ours. What do you think?"

My heart takes a massive surge. I was confused on a conscious level, since he had abruptly and completely changed our conversation topic. And she is not even here; she is in her basket at the maternity ward. The staff is able to care for her during the day.

We have a whole new level of respect for the night needs of a premature baby. We have been taking turns getting up when she cries or when the heat alarm sounds. I have experienced the shock twice in my sleepy, barefoot state when touching the metal base. Georgette seems to like to be awake all night and sleep during the day.

On a subconscious level, Rich's question is the yearning of my heart, although I have never expressed it to him. I take a deep breath to tame my excitement. "I would love it. I know we talked before getting married about how much we both want children. And there is the uncertainty of my ability to bear my own children. Do you feel like she is supposed to be ours?"

"Yes, I do. I have been praying about it. I don't know what our families will say or even what we'd have to do. I guess we would have to make sure Georgette's family doesn't think they can take care of her."

I throw my arms around his neck. My heart is bursting open. I haven't allowed myself to entertain the possibility. I'm deeply emotionally bonded to Georgette, and I love her. The thought of ever leaving her is unfathomable. In that instant, although I don't know how, I know she'll be ours.

*    *    *    *

The next several days are a flurry of activity. We ask for advice from Dr. Hodges, and especially Barbara, who has gone through the process of adopting five orphans with special needs for Doctor and Joanna. We bring our decision up as a prayer request during the weekly bible study. We write letters home to get the reaction of our families.

I journal even more than just the daily events; I now reflect emotionally about what adoption could mean. I consider how ironic it would be for us to have a child by adoption, since I was adopted at the age of nine myself. I know I am forever grateful for the family that changed the trajectory of my life and provided me with hope in uncertain times. The wee one and I would have another common thread.

The first action is to get permission from the family, even though they have stated their intention to leave her for the orphan nursery. Madame Rafael has family from the same area where Georgette's family lives. She sends word to have Assondier return to the hospital.

When he arrives, Assondier is not alone. There are many family members with him. At first, my heart sinks and I think, *What if they have decided to keep her? Lord, your will be done.*

Barbara is much more fluent in Creole so she translates for us. "Monsieur and Madame Rich are interested in adopting your baby girl if you still intend to leave her for the orphanage."

In Creole, Assondier says, "We have decided to leave her with the hospital and know you will do what you feel is best. I'm not able to care for her properly."

"Will you want to take her when she is older and stronger?"

"Our decision is to keep her here."

"Your decision doesn't need to be made today. Preliminary papers are needed. For example, have you already gotten a death certificate from the magistrate of your village where Madame Assondier is buried?"

"No. I did not get a death certificate." Still, a broad grin breaks across his face. "I'd be happy and honored if they take the baby."

"Also, there will be no money in exchange for the baby."

"I understand."

"And one more thing, Monsieur and Madame Rich may be returning to the United States and will not be raising the baby here in Haiti. Will you still be in agreement?"

Intently, I watch the faces of Assondier and the family. They begin to speak rapidly with each other, and there are smiles on their faces.

Finally, Assondier turns to Rich and me and says, "We would be honored for you to have the baby. We understand you may leave and return to the United States. The baby will have a better life there."

My heart takes another leap. Their decision is more confirmation that this is the right choice for us to make.

Barbara tells Assondier, "Papers will need to be signed, so we will send for you to come when they are ready."

Now he looks concerned, displaying a deep furrowed brow and speaking rapidly to Barbara.

*Could he change his mind that quickly?*

Searching Barbara's face for an explanation as she is speaking to him, she finally translates for us saying, "He is concerned, since he does not read or write, how he will sign the papers. I told him he can make an *X* and someone can witness it for him. He's good with that."

*       *       *       *

Several days later, Barbara lets us know there is a lawyer in Cap-Haïtien who has helped with two of their adoptions. He is interested in helping us complete the adoption. He apparently wants to see as many children escape this country as possible. Our concern is for money, as we are serving here as volunteers and have used most of our savings for our support. She assures us that he will be reasonable.

One of the necessary items is a picture of Georgette for the paperwork. She's so small that getting a passport-sized picture is quite a challenge. An official photographer in Cap-Haïtien finally accomplishes the task.

I make a trip to the village of Camp Coq, where Georgette's family resides, and meet with the magistrate about the death certificate. He agrees to write the paper for a price of five American dollars. I sit in a woven chair in a small and dark Haitian mud-and-wattle hut with a thatched roof. The magistrate begins the process of handwriting a lengthy document in French. When he has completed about half of it, he stops and asks me for more money. I agree, as I can see there is a lot of work going into the creation of the certificate. He writes more and puts the pen down again and requests more money. By this time, I am getting frustrated but agree. This happens again and I've had enough.

"You told me the price when you started and now you have changed it three times. If you cannot produce the certificate for fifteen American dollars, then I'll leave without it."

"But you need the death certificate."

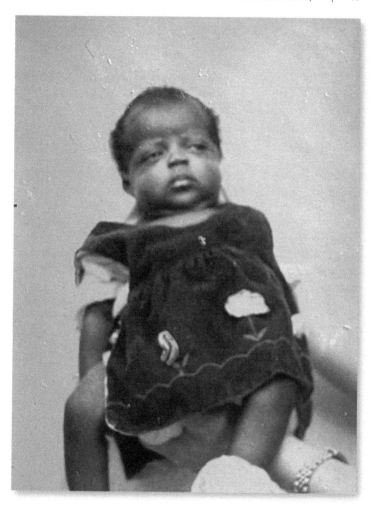

"I am sure I'll find someone else to produce the document. Since she officially died in Limbé, I'll speak with the magistrate there. I'm sure he will be happy to have the fifteen dollars I've agreed to pay you." Getting up and moving outside into the bright sunshine, I am not sure if he'll take my bluff, but I am happy to be out of the hut's stale air.

He runs after me, "Madame. I'll do it for fifteen dollars. It's a lot of work to write this paper for you."

"I'll have the magistrate in Limbé do it."

"But I have already done this much work and you have not paid me anything."

"And you changed your price three times and I have no paper. So, what will it be? No money and no paper, or fifteen dollars and you finish the death certificate?"

"I'll finish."

The truth is, that's the only money that I have with me. Barbara told me five dollars would be sufficient. I came prepared with a little extra, in case. My confidence in coming alone is a bit shaky, but I am determined to get everything in order for the adoption. After three hours of swatting at flies and listening to the crescendo and decrescendo of the cicadas, I have a handwritten paper which supposedly says that Madame Assondier is, indeed, dead. I do not understand French, so I have to trust that he has done what is legally necessary.

I recognize something from the papers. Madame Assonier's given name is Elirose; my middle name is also Rose. I don't think this is a coincidence. For me, it is another reassurance. Georgette's biological mother was also the same age as me.

I snap out of my musings as the man thanks me for coming up the mountain and for what we are doing for the baby. He seems happy with his payday. I depart and we're friends.

*   *   *   *

On occasion, we have an opportunity to call home. It is quite an undertaking. We have to have a ride to Cap-Haïtien when one of the vehicles is going there. With all the political upheaval, there are often roadblocks made of tires across the road, occasionally set on fire. Usually, there are armed individuals—some as young as teenage boys—with automatic weapons. Portions of the main paved road are in poor repair as there are no initiatives to maintain the roads. With the torrential downpours and hurricanes that Haiti is victim to, sections of the road are completely washed away.

The road leads out of Limbé, crosses the Limbé River, and winds its way up a mountain and down into a plain where the beautiful Bay of Acul can be seen. There are rice fields in the low lands. On the side of the mountains, we can see terraced gardens that the peasant farmers tend for beans and other produce. Since many fields are on such a steep incline, the clinic has received farmers with broken bones who have fallen off their garden. The farmers work their land with hand tools, usually a hoe and a machete.

As the road nears the second largest city in Haiti, we see occasional evidence of nice, large, block homes along the road. The dichotomy between the mud-and-wattle, thatched-roof huts and the well-built homes demonstrates the drastic extremes evident in Haiti. The "haves" and the "have-nots." There is an elite class of educated and prosperous Haitians and then there are peasants, with seemingly few in the middle.

To get to the Teleco, where international phone calls can be made, we ride through the dusty streets of Cap-Haïtien. There are throngs of people making their way around on foot. There are muscular men wheeling carts, with any variety of contents, in a way others would use an animal to pull the carts.

At the Teleco, there are lines of people waiting to make calls. We give our name and the number we want to call and then we wait. Along one wall, there is a bench crowded with people. After nearly two hours of standing, we are offered a place on the bench. Another forty-five minutes pass and we are finally motioned to a booth with a phone. Our call is connected and it sounds like we are on the other side of the Earth.

We are making a call to Rich's family to discuss the adoption decision we have made. We have already written to them but have not received a response yet. We barely have the opportunity to greet them when the power goes out. In the darkened building with only two windows, chaos erupts. People begin yelling, upset they have lost calls or haven't been able to make them. We wait to see what is going to happen next. Blackouts are a common occurrence and can last a few minutes to days. Suddenly, a man is at our booth and tells us we are going to have to leave. They are closing the Teleco and no more calls can be made today.

Upset and frustrated like many around us, we leave the building. I begin to get apprehensive that this blackout and disruption of communication has political implications. Tension seems high among the people in the streets. I am sure we need to return to the relative safety of the mission compound in Limbé. We have no way of communicating with our family to tell them what is happening.

\*    \*    \*    \*

afely back at the mission, we meet with Barbara, who has good news for us. The initial paperwork to take to the magistrate in Limbé is ready for Assondier and his witness to sign. She has sent for them and expects they will arrive soon.

Two days later, while I am working in the surgical ward, Jacques finds me. "Madame Rich, the baby's family is here for the papers. Miss Barbara has asked that I have you come to the office."

My heart is doing a happy dance. *Can it be? This is going to happen?* I round the corner by the office and see a crowd of thirteen people. Assondier, Rich, and Barbara are standing on the walkway in front of the office door talking. My elated smile expresses the joy I can't contain. After greeting Assondier, who is dressed in his Sunday's best, I ask, "Who are all these people?" Looking closer, I see the grandmothers and a few faces I recognize from the time Georgette's mother was in the hospital.

"This is my family, and they want to give their approval for you to have the baby, too." He introduces everyone and I shake each person's hand. They seem hesitant with the handshake custom.

"Well," Barbara says, "I've sent a worker ahead of us to the magistrate to let him know we're coming. Shall we go?"

We make quite an unusual scene as our group walks through the muddy roads of Limbé to the small office of the magistrate. Three *blancs* and a well-dressed group of peasant Haitians walking and talking together get the attention of people on the road and their porches. They call out to our group to know what is happening. Several give a short explanation that the "blanc missionaries are adopting our baby."

By the time we arrive at the magistrate's office, a crowd has joined us, not wanting to miss any excitement. Barbara tells them, "You can go on home; there's nothing to see here. We are only taking care of paperwork." Most are undeterred and choose to stay.

Inside of the office, there is only room for four of us at a time. It is getting dark outside and there is a single kerosene lamp on the counter. A heavyset man is behind the counter. He has generous, round cheeks and a pair of black-framed glasses sit askew on his flat nose. He asks Assondier a series of questions and Barbara translates for us.

"Why are you giving these people your baby? Have they paid you money for the baby? Are you sure you no longer want any rights for the baby? Has any coercion been used to force you to make this decision?"

Although he looks nervous and his forehead is glistening with sweat, Assondier answers each question with conviction.

Addressing us, Barbara translates for the magistrate. "Are you prepared to care for this baby as parents? Do you understand that you are not to pay this man or anyone in his family for this child?"

Answering his questions affirmatively, we wait for him to write on a paper.

The room is stuffy and the body odor is pungent. I remind myself to keep breathing as we watch the next part of the proceeding. Finally, the magistrate turns the paper to Assondier and hands him a pen. Assondier looks at us and his mother. Taking the pen, he places the tip on the paper where the man is pointing. He looks uncertain and happy at the same time. He makes an *X* on the paper next to where his name has been printed. "I want to do it right."

The magistrate requests an uncle to sign his name as Assondier's witness. Next, it is our turn to sign the paper. I am aware of the pounding of my heart in my chest as I am given the blue Bic pen to sign this declaration of our intent to take a child as our own.

With the formalities complete, I want to jump and skip back to the mission compound. Barbara cautions us with reality. "This is only a part of the process, you understand. This transaction needs to be approved by the courts in Cap-Haïtien. You will also have much work to get a visa for her to be able to come to the States with you, if you do not stay here. Legally, she is not yours yet."

"How long will the rest of this take . . . the adoption?"

"This is Haiti. It could be months, even a year."

Still, I know we are on the path, and it is so exciting. Returning to the maternity ward, I retrieve sleeping Georgette from her basket and bring her out for the family to say goodbye. Her maternal grandmother says, "See? I said she was your baby."

A big grin stretches across my face, "Yes, you did. You certainly did."

# Chapter Fifteen

surgery team will be coming in from the States next week. All the preparations are coming together. Today, I'm holding a surgery triage in the courtyard of the hospital. The radio station 4VEH has announced the surgical team arrival and people are coming from all around to have tumors, hernias, and many other surgical needs evaluated.

I've seen one of the largest thyroid masses ever. One young boy has a basketball-sized mass on his upper thigh, which may be a sarcoma—a deadly cancer. A woman in her early twenties has a massive ovarian tumor that makes her look ten months pregnant. She's happy that she will be having it removed. She has been begging for money in Cap-Haïtien in order to have surgery. I hand out tickets and assign dates and times. All major surgeries will cost eighty dollars and must be paid in advance. That price will cover all the surgical supplies, personnel, dressings, medications, IV fluids, and follow-up visits.

In the midst of my makeshift triage—located in the courtyard between the adult medical ward and the maternity ward—I see Barbara walk up the steps and into the office. She went to Cap-Haïtien early today to handle business. She promised to stop at the lawyer's office to see if anything has been done with Georgette's adoption papers. We've been continuing to care for her at home during the nights. The maternity nurses cared for her during the daytime hours with her woven-basket bed inside the corner crib until about a week ago. At that time, Madame Edmond stopped me one morning on my way to the hospital. I have a dark-blue corduroy infant carrier loaned to me from another mission family that I wear on the front of me. Georgette is still so small you can't see her head, only her legs sticking out the bottom openings. As Madame Edmond peered inside the carrier, she told me she wanted to take care of Georgette while we're at work. We agreed that she would still do her other duties. She adores the baby. She insisted that she be permitted to use the wearable infant carrier, too. Madame Edmond and Georgette make quite a pair.

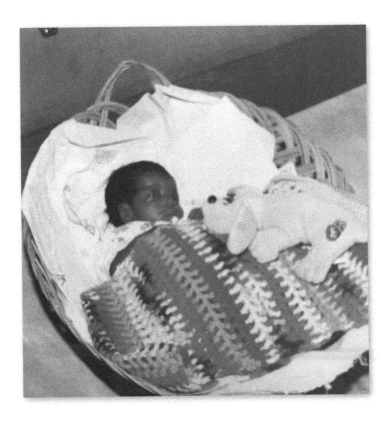

In the courtyard, I distribute sixty tickets and tell several others to come back next week. If there are people who do not come for their surgery or if the team is able to do more, the others will have a chance. I'm a little anxious for the whole process. It's difficult to decide who gets a chance. I am making decisions for surgeons who will not see their patients until they arrive for the surgery that I schedule. I hope next week will go as I envision it—having never done anything like this before. We have two surgical rooms set up, one for major surgery and one for minor surgery only requiring local anesthetics. We don't have an anesthesia machine or the continuous monitors like in the States, but I have been told the surgical group is bringing those as well as a cautery machine to control bleeding.

As I gather my papers together, Barbara saunters over to me. She has been in Haiti most of her life and moves at island speed most of the time. She has also been having a lot of problems with joint pain and no explanation can be found.

"Sheri, I have news for you and Rich. You'll want to hear it together."

"Good or bad news?"

She only chuckles and says, "Let's go over to the pharmacy office."

As I follow her, I realize there's a folder in her hand. I don't know whether to be excited or concerned. This process has had its ups and downs; we complete a form only to need another one. We find Rich at the desk in the back pharmacy office. He looks up as we enter.

Barbara says, "As you know, I stopped by the lawyer's office while I was in town this morning taking care of other business."

I wait impatiently. She talks like she walks, never in a hurry. But she does seem to have a twinkle in her eye.

Laying the folder on the desk in front of us, she opens it and says, "Congratulations. You are the parents of Georgette Ruth Remy Roby."

Speechless. My brain cannot even form a word, let alone a question. Barbara laughs as she looks at our dumbfounded faces.

"Oh, but . . ." The words are swirling in my head and attempting to make sense of what she said. "I thought it was going to take months. Aren't we supposed to go to court for this?"

Rich is equally stunned but is all smiles. "Are you sure? It's official?"

"Yes, it's complete and it's official. You did not have to go to court because you signed a paper allowing the lawyer to be your power of attorney to represent you in court. He was able to expedite the whole process. He desires to see children adopted by families."

Finally, the reality sinks into my heart and happy tears cannot be restrained. Rich moves around the desk and gives me a great, big hug. We all exchange hugs and thank Barbara. I sit down on a folding chair and try to comprehend the magnitude of what has happened.

"We have a baby." I bounce from the chair and know I need to tell the world. "I am going to maternity to tell the nurses."

As I rush out the door, Faith, a nurse volunteer who oversees the pediatric ward, is about to enter. "We have a baby! Georgette is ours!" I throw my arms around her in a big embrace and we dance around, making a scene. Faith and I were roommates for a while when I was here previously. We shared many late-night talks about life and family. She heard the longings of my heart to be married to Rich, whom I had met in 1984 when he also came to the hospital from Ohio as a volunteer. He returned home after his one-year term while I stayed on for a second term.

After the overthrow of "Baby Doc" Jean-Claude Duvalier in February 1986, Haiti was complete chaos in the political power vacuum. At that time, we were cut off from the world with no way to communicate with people at home. We were not permitted to leave the compound for safety reasons and there was talk of evacuating all the Americans. Rich and I wrote long letters to each other every week, but during that time, there was no way to get the mail in or out of the country. Finally, an official visited the compound and said he would find a way to get our mail out of the country. I quickly wrote a note to Rich telling him I would find a way to get to Florida for my birthday in April—I could stay with family there. If he received the letter and wanted to see me, I hoped he would find a way to Florida.

As it turned out, we both were able to make it to Florida and had a wonderful ten days to visit and see the sights. It was quite the reverse culture shock of being in Haiti. The most exciting event was one evening while Rich and I were taking pictures of ourselves. I wanted to have pictures to take back with me when I returned to Haiti. After getting six or eight different poses, Rich had asked me to set the timer for one more. At the moment the timer went off, he revealed a ring for me to see. The picture was priceless. The happiness I felt then was akin to what I was feeling right this moment.

Suddenly, it seemed everyone was around us—volunteers, missionaries, and Haitian staff. Somebody asked, "Well, where is your new daughter?"

"I should go get her." My feet barely touch the walk as I fly to our house. "Madame Edmond, the baby is ours! The adoption is complete. Where is Georgette?"

"She ate and fell asleep."

"That is why she stays up all night for us. I am going to take her over to the hospital for a little bit for everyone to see us together."

Taking her out of the incubator, she awakens and looks up at me with those beautiful eyes. In that instant, a minute becomes a lifetime.

"Hi, baby girl. I'm your new mommy."

# Chapter Sixteen

The mail is here. The cage-covered pickup truck pulls into the hospital yard. The volunteers and missionaries who did not go with the rest of the group to the beach descend on the truck to help unload and distribute the mail and packages. After a productive week of eighty-five surgeries, the surgical team also left this morning.

I am walking with Georgette in the infant carrier. She weighs six-and-a-half pounds. We have been working on getting a visa for her so she can travel with us to the States next month for the holidays with our family. We will be making a trip to Port-au-Prince for the final arrangements in the next several weeks.

"Hi, Sheri and Georgette. You are in time to get your mail. Another care box from home. You certainly have good support at home."

Smiling, I respond to Barbara who made the trip to Agape Fights to retrieve our precious items. "Yes, we're abundantly blessed."

I balance the box under one arm, the mail in my other hand, and Georgette snuggled in front of me; we make quite a scene walking back to the house. Rich sees us coming and hurries to help carry the box. Getting to the house, he begins to sort through the letters and opens the box. There are a few goodies for us and many more items for Georgette, including cute little dresses, plastic bottles, toys, and diapers.

"It's funny, there's a lot less for us now that we have a baby."

"I guess we know who's important here. And I'm so thankful for these things for her. Look at this adorable little red dress with white ruffles." Putting the dress down, I move to the other room to take Georgette out of the carrier and strap her in the bouncy chair loaned to us.

Rich has a cassette of Christian praise music playing and Georgette seems to connect with the music. Her little arms and feet wave around.

"Look, she's clapping her feet in sync with the music." Rich joins me and squats down in front of her to coo at her while I prepare a bottle. Getting her to drink is no longer a problem. If anything, we can barely keep up with her demand.

There have been many late-night and early-morning pacing walks through the living and dining rooms to lull her to sleep. We no longer use the incubator. A soft, yellow baby hammock with a pocket for a plastic battery-operated heart that emits a soothing heartbeat hangs across the top of her crib. We moved her crib from our bedroom after the first few nights; no one was sleeping.

I'm still adjusting to the thought of motherhood. While some people have an unplanned pregnancy, we had an unplanned adoption. And while most mothers have nine months to prepare for motherhood, our journey has been much shorter. I have no qualms about having an adopted child. I was an adopted child at the older age of nine. I am forever grateful to my adoptive parents for the life they gave me, that I would not have experienced otherwise. *It's the circle of life—with a twist.*

Rich begins reading letters at the table on the screened porch while I rock and feed Georgette in the living room. After a little while, I hear his chair scrape the cement floor. He appears in the doorway and, immediately, I know something is wrong. His eyes are red rimmed, his face flushed, and he's clenching his jaw muscles. He's holding a letter in his hand at his side.

"What's the matter? You look upset."

He's so distressed he doesn't even speak. Handing the letter to me, he takes Georgette from me to finish the feeding.

The handwritten letter is from a family member. As I read the words, disappointment begins to flood my soul. This person wants us to know that our decision to adopt cross-racially and cross-culturally is not being accepted well at home. Apparently, the timing of our letters crossed in the mail. The time span between making the decision to adopt and then it becoming a reality was such so short. It feels like someone just kicked me in the chest.

I begin to cry. "She's gone through so much. We felt so sure of God's will for us, concerning her. How can it be that we don't have their support?"

"I don't know. Maybe it's too much, too fast?"

"But it sounds like they can't handle the idea of having a child of color in the family. Living in Haiti, we understand what it means to be the minority. I don't even see color. People are people. I want Georgette to be accepted as a child—Georgette—not a Black child. Not a Haitian child. Only our baby daughter who we love."

Taking Georgette with me, I lay down on the bed with her curled up next to me. I cry myself to sleep for a late afternoon nap.

*    *    *    *

A few days later, after a lot of prayer and discussion, I write a letter in response to the one we received and address it to the family members. In it, I explain our position of feeling led to go through with our unplanned adoption. I diplomatically approach the subject of the feasibility of raising a Black child in a White family. I point out that if we are indeed to come back to the States, it will be necessary for us to have the support of our loved ones to accomplish the task successfully. I also let them know we are moving forward with the efforts to get her visa in time for us to visit home at Christmas as a family.

We received a different letter the same day, from another part of our family, saying how excited they were and asking for pictures of the newest family member. It's interesting how the negative letter overshadowed the joy of the other one. We are choosing joy over discouragement. I also answer their letter, including a copy of the Georgette's passport picture that we had taken for her visa. I'm excited knowing that someone will be proudly showing off Georgette.

*Monday, December 12, 1988*

# Chapter Seventeen

R ich and I are riding along the main road to Port-au-Prince with a business acquaintance of the hospital. We've finally gotten the needed paperwork to present to the embassy to request a visa for Georgette. I have her wrapped up in blankets in my arms. We don't have a car seat. I'm grateful we're not riding in a camion—the large buses, and the common transportation, throughout the country. I can't imagine what that would be like traveling with the baby. The camion may be the return transportation we get, depending on what happens while we are in Port-au-Prince.

Several of the volunteers offered to take over our tasks so we can make this trip. Additional short-term volunteers are expected while we go home over the holidays. We have discussed at length what we should do with Georgette. I can't imagine leaving her here while we go to the States, although several people have offered to take care of her if we are not able to get the visa. We don't have much time since we are to leave next week, on December 19. So far, the doors have opened one by one, and we keep stepping through in faith. We still feel a bit of uncertainty about how Georgette will be accepted if we are able to take her with us.

After many stops at roadblocks explaining our intentions, we consider it nothing less than a miracle to make it to Port-au-Prince. It is the afternoon, even though we left early in the morning. What should have taken us no more than three or four hours took us eight hours. We're dropped off at a school run by a Catholic nun. Barbara has given us a letter of introduction and a request that we be given a room to stay while we carry out our business.

We are shown to an upstairs room with a red tile floor, a single bed, and a bathroom down the hall. We are told the meal times and where to go. We have a new diaper-changing pad that folds into a bag with straps that has places for bottles and diapers. This becomes Georgette's bed. We enjoy a meal with the school staff and share what we have been through and what we hope to accomplish. We are given helpful insight of what to expect tomorrow at the embassy. Georgette gets a lot of attention from everyone and thrives on it.

As we return to our room, I am feeling excited. Everything will be done tomorrow and we'll be ready for our trip home as a family. The door to our room has barely closed when we hear "rat-a-tat-tat" from right outside our second-floor window. Then, there are guns being fired. Quickly, we huddle together on the floor next to the bed and away from the window, as much as possible. The gunfire is intermittent, sometimes close and other times more distant. Sleep is elusive for us, but Georgette sleeps through the night for the first time ever.

# Chapter Eighteen

The next morning, we leave the school and make our way on foot through the dusty, pungent streets of Port-au-Prince to the American Embassy. We are shocked to see Haitians lined for a block and a half from the door. We're not sure what to do. It appears we'll be waiting in the heat and sun for hours if we join at the end of the line. I decide to see if we can get in at the front of the line since we are Americans, or if there is another door for us to enter; this is not a wise decision. A few Haitians standing toward the front of the line yell angrily at us to go to the end of the line.

We are not prepared to stand here all day with the baby. We have been assured that she must be with us for the processing. We consider having one of us go back to the school with the baby while the other waits, but there is no guarantee how quickly the line will move. We decide to stay together.

At about 3:00 p.m., an armed guard walks back along the line and tells us all to leave. All that will be seen for the day have already entered. I am hot, tired, thirsty, and frustrated. And keeping Georgette distracted and happy has been less than pleasant all day. I motion to the guard. He seems shocked to see us standing in the line.

"Why are you here?"

"We are Americans, and this is our adopted daughter. We are to get her visa. The paperwork is already here."

"No, I mean, why are you in this line?"

"This is where we were told to be."

"Come with me."

We follow the guard to a side door and are ushered into a small room with three closed frosted-glass windows. The guard steps through a dark wooden door at the end of the room as we gratefully take a seat on a wooden bench. Georgette is fussy and we don't have any more formula with us. There are also other people sitting and waiting in the room.

Suddenly, one of the frosted windows opens and we are motioned to come to the window. "State the reason for your visit."

I do my best to respond in Creole, wishing that Barbara would have come with us.

"Explain to me in English," says the tall, slender Haitian man.

"We have sent a dossier of papers for our adopted daughter, Georgette Roby. We are to get her visa." I show him copies of the adoption papers, which have been translated from French to English.

He studies them for a moment and looks at me and says, "You can't get a visa for her today. You'll have to come back tomorrow."

"Please Sir, we can't stand in the heat and sun with our little baby another day like we have today."

"Come back tomorrow."

"What kind of guarantee is there for getting the visa then?"

"No guarantee. Come back tomorrow."

I am angry and frustrated. We leave with Rich carrying Georgette. We pass armed guards and others with guns. Given our exhaustion and need to get back to the school as quickly as possible, I wave down a car that I believe to be a taxi.

Giving the driver the name of the school and the road, he agrees to take us. We barter the price to be two dollars. Almost as soon as we are in the car, I get an uneasy feeling. The driver begins to take us in a direction farther from the school. He assures me it is the way. After driving up and down roads for a while, he stops the car and asks for more money. I am not in any mood for these kinds of games.

"Take us to the school for the price you already agreed to or we will get out now and there will be no money."

Under his breath, Rich says, "This could be dangerous for us. Don't make him mad."

The driver says he is not a taxi, and he will not take us any further without more money. "We'll walk from here, then." I decide to give him the money only because I don't want an enemy. We get out of the car and try to get our bearings for which direction we believe the school to be.

By the time we finally arrive at the school, we have missed dinner and are exhausted. The nun instructs the helper to get us leftover food from the kitchen. Taking it to our room, we get Georgette a bottle and collapse on the bed. Not even the gunfire can keep me awake tonight.

*Wednesday, December 14, 1988*

# Chapter Nineteen

Before leaving for the embassy early the next morning, Rich and I pray for God's hand of protection and guidance. We ask that all the people who are needed to accomplish this goal will be present and willing to assist us today. Even though everything is so uncertain in this country, I have a sense of peace. I know we are in the center of God's will.

The nun has arranged a ride to take us to the embassy and the driver is waiting for us in the front office. As we arrive at the embassy, I notice the guard from yesterday. Recognizing us, he asks us to wait to the side of the line and speaks with another guard who enters the building. About an hour passes and we are beginning to wonder if this will be a repeat of yesterday. Thankfully, we are more prepared today for a long wait with food, water, and extra formula for Georgette. We're wearing yesterday's clothes since we did not expect to have this kind of a delay in Port-au-Prince. The line of Haitians is moving forward while we remain to the side in the shade of the building.

Finally, the guard who entered the building returns and speaks to the guard we have gotten to know, Philipé. He asks us to follow him. Stepping inside a hallway from the bright sunlight, we take a moment for our eyes to adjust. There's a long line of Haitians, speaking in hushed tones while they wait. The guard asks people to step aside and let us pass. Part of me feels grateful that we are enjoying forward progress; the other part of me feels guilty for being treated differently because of the color of our skin or our nationality. Ahead of us, there is a ramp that leads up to a series of windows on the left.

The guard places us next in line and says, "They will take care of you now. Tell them your name and the baby's name. Thank you for taking that small baby as your own. You will give her a better life."

"Thank you, Philipé, for all you've done for us."

He turns and is gone. The person in front of us completes his business and we present our request for Georgette's visa, again showing our papers. The man looks at the papers and then looks at us. I hold Georgette up for him to be able to see her. She is awake and taking in all activity.

"Wait here." He leaves his chair and passes through a door behind the chairs. After another ten-minute wait, my confidence is beginning to erode. The people behind us are complaining louder about the time our transaction is taking.

Finally, the man reappears and has a large yellow envelope. He opens it and shakes out the contents. He asks us a few questions, places a form to sign in a security drawer that he extends to us. We both sign the form and he retrieves it. We see him stamp something and, again, extends the security drawer. There it is. In my hand, I'm holding a navy-blue passport with gold-embossed lettering, "République D'Haiti, Passeport," and the Haitian seal of arms. I can hardly believe the journey we have taken to get to this moment.

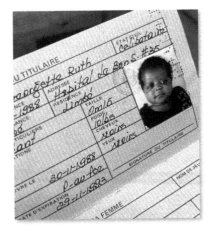

＊     ＊     ＊     ＊

We return to the school and the nun tells us they have been praying for us. Together, we sit down and say a prayer of thanks. Then she asks, "What are your plans for your return trip to Limbé?"

Rich and I look at each other as Georgette begins to cry in his arms. "We didn't make a plan for that since we didn't know how long this would take. The person who brought us has already returned to the north yesterday. Maybe we can get a ride to the camion station."

"You shouldn't take the baby on a camion. That'll be too difficult for her and for you. Let me see if I can find anyone with business to complete in the north who may be going that way in the next several days."

"We are grateful, but we cannot take any more time away from the hospital, especially since we are to be gone over the holidays."

"I understand. Go freshen up for dinner and I'll see you in a little while."

Returning to our room, we pack up the few things we have with us in preparation for leaving. Taking Georgette to see her many new friends, we join several nuns and others for dinner. Georgette gets passed around and is quite the socialite. To the delight of one nun with many age creases and laugh lines, Georgette coos and excitedly kicks her feet and waves her arm.

"That is her victory pose," I say. Everyone laughs and Georgette responds with more cooing noises.

The director nun comes into the room with a smile on her face. "I have great news for you. I have a trusted driver who'll be going to the north in the morning. He's happy to have company and will take you. And his car is air conditioned so you will all be much more comfortable."

"God does provide."

# Chapter Twenty

"I know we have much to do to be ready to leave on Monday, but I have repeatedly promised Madame Abner that we would visit her new house in Limbé. Let's take some time this evening to do that."

"Should we take Georgette or is this our first experience getting a babysitter so we can go out?" Rich chuckles.

"She will go with us, of course. It is only fitting that Adlin and Georgette meet. I'll send word with Jacques to let her know we will come."

At dusk, we are met at the compound gate by Madame Abner. She's wearing a beautiful blue chiffon dress and jelly sandals, and she can't help but nearly skip. Her excitement is contagious. We walk along the dusty road and in between cramped dwellings. Rounding the corner, a happy, pudgy-faced two year old appears. He throws his hands up. "Momma!"

Madame Abner scoops Adlin up and twirls him around. "See who I brought to visit you?"

Adlin has a toothy smile behind big lips. He puts his hand out to me.

"Do you remember me, Adlin?" I ask.

A vigorous shake of his head and he squirms to get down on the ground.

Proudly, Madame Abner introduces us to neighbors and others who are milling around for the excitement. "Come in and see our home and what I did to it."

Abner appears with a kerosene lamp and greets us. He leads the way as we peer into their mud-and-wattle hut. Urging us to enter all the way, Madame Abner eagerly shows us her handiwork. The main room we are in is about six-by-eight feet. To the back, there's a second, smaller room where it appears all their belongings have been stacked. On the walls are newspapers—the colorful and shiny advertisement pages.

"Where did you—"

"Madame Doctor told me I could have the packing paper from boxes of instruments and supplies." She is so excited. She grabs my hands and dances around in a circle. Rich is holding Georgette, who is taking it all in. Adlin joins in the circle to dance with us. *How happy they are with so little.*

# Chapter Twenty-One

As a family, Rich, Georgette, and I walk through the door to our apartment outside of Columbus, Ohio. A family member has been staying in our apartment while we serve in Haiti. The last couple of days have been travel and opportunity to see family in Florida. Georgette has been well received and everyone loves her. Before leaving Haiti, we received a couple of letters from family who had expressed concern. They had assured us of their love and support of whatever decisions we felt were necessary. They also asked us to be patient with them since we are surrounded by the Haitian culture, and it may take time to adjust to the idea.

Georgette's new cousins are smitten with her and dance around in excitement to finally see the baby we have been writing about in our letters. Finally, her new carrier is placed on the table for everyone to see her. Rich's dad, a tall, strong man with work-hardened hands, lifts her out of the carrier. Holding her in front of him in his hands, face-to-face with her, he says, "Don't think you are going to wrap me around your little finger."

Too late. It's already done.

# Afterword

I n the years that have passed since Georgette's adoption, there have been many life events. We returned to Haiti after our Christmas break to finish our one-year term in early August 1989. We anticipated future opportunities to return to the country as long-term missionaries, however, that did not happen. Georgette gained a brother, Trevor—our biological miracle—when she was three-and-a-half years old.

Together, as a family, we had the opportunity to travel to Hôpital Bon Samaritain on a couple of occasions. Georgette was nearly five years old when we went back for the first time, and twelve years old on the second trip. During both of those visits, we were able to see Georgette's biological family. Georgette also had the opportunity to work in the orphan nursery—now named Kia Mira—during the second trip.

Georgette is now a graduate of Ohio Northern University, with a degree in vocal music performance. One of the most poignant moments for me occurred on February 4, 2010, at Ohio Northern. Georgette had responded to the devastating Haiti earthquake that hit three weeks prior by organizing and performing in a musical and artistic benefit to raise money for Haiti. As the slideshow of the devastation of Port-au-Prince played on a screen behind her, Georgette sang her heart out for her native country. My mind remembered the prophecy spoken by the nurse long ago: "Someday, this little baby will be a big testimony for God."

# Acknowledgements

I am deeply grateful to Nadia Geagea Pupa and Lindsay Denney for their editing and publishing expertise. The continual encouragement and guidance from Nadia is the only reason this manuscript is not still tucked away in a binder on a shelf. I also wish to thank Laurie Dufresne, not only for making the introduction to your amazing and talented niece, Nadia, but for your ongoing mentorship and encouragement for me to dream bigger.

I owe a special debt of gratitude to an influential high school English teacher, the late Helen Romano, who told me decades ago that I would write and publish a book—at least one. I'm thankful to Sara DeFord who saw something special in me that I could not see myself when she awarded me a full scholarship to attend Lake Erie College. Both she and a dear friend and research librarian, Phyllis—whose last name escapes me, but whose impact I have remembered always—taught me the value of paying it forward. While both of you have been welcomed into your eternal rest, your legacy lives on in part through me.

Although Dr. William (Bill), Joanna Hodges, and their daughter, Barbara, have also passed on, their lives devoted to service and love for the people of Haiti has had a profound lifelong effect on me. A sincere thank you to Dr. Steve and Nancy James for your godly example and loving guidance of me as a young, idealistic volunteer and new mother. Thank you to Rich Roby, for the journey we shared together and for your fatherly role.

My deepest thanks goes to my family. To my dear husband, Mike, thank you for loving me, understanding my need to share this story, and encouraging me to finish writing it. I'm grateful for the broken road that brought us together and for the bonus daughters, Alison and Emma, and their families that we get to love together.

Karen Jeske, you took me in, loved and believed in me, and always encouraged me to seek my own path. You are truly the best mom I could ever have been blessed with and I love you forever. You and Dad, Al Jeske, taught me the best definition of family isn't always biological—it's love. And finally, a very special thank you to my children, Georgette and Trevor. You're so very different and beautifully unique in your own ways, yet both miracles and God's greatest gift to me. I love you both with my whole heart.

# *About the Author*

Sheri Gentry is a skilled storyteller and speaker. Her love of the power of words began at a young age and has been a valuable asset in her roles as a physician assistant, professional health coach, former medical missionary volunteer in Haiti, midwife, and university assistant professor. Sheri is strong in her faith. She embraces obstacles as opportunities and sees the adventure in adversity.

Sheri and her husband, Mike, live on a quiet farm in Northwest Ohio. They have four grown children, two living granddaughters, two in heaven, two dogs, and two horses. Sheri enjoys woodworking and water activities as her hobbies.

For speaking inquires, please send an email to *gentrywellness@gmail.com* or visit *www.GentryWellness.com.*

Scan this QR code to watch Sheri's video about transformation and empowerment.

GentryWellness.com

CPSIA information can be obtained
at www.ICGtesting.com
Printed in the USA
LVHW020711030622
720419LV00011B/105

9 780578 331010